THE IDEA OF HOLINESS AND
THE HUMANE RESPONSE

The Idea of Holiness
and the
Humane Response

*A study of the concept of holiness
and its social consequences*

JOHN ARMSTRONG

London
GEORGE ALLEN & UNWIN
Boston   Sydney

GEORGE ALLEN & UNWIN LTD
40 Museum Street, London WC1A 1LU

ᶜ John Armstrong, 1981

British Library Cataloguing in Publication Data

Armstrong, John H S
    The idea of holiness and the humane response.
    1. Holiness   2. Bible. *Old Testament* —
    Commentaries
    I. Title
    234'.1   BT767

    ISBN 0-04-200042-4

Typeset in 11 on 13 point Garamond by
Alan Sutton Ltd, Gloucester
and printed in Great Britain
by Billing and Sons Ltd, Guildford,
London and Worcester.

ACKNOWLEDGEMENTS

I should like to thank a number of people without whose help the writing of this book would have been insuperably daunting. In particular, I am most grateful to Professor P. Brockbank for very kindly arranging my visiting fellowship at the University of York, so giving me time for research and writing, but in the context of a scholarly fraternity. I also wish warmly to thank Professors R.B. Dobson and R.H. Hilton for generous and indispensable advice on reading, as regards the Middle Ages. My greatest debt of all is to Mrs. J.E. Reed, who with wonderful patience and accuracy deciphered and typed successive versions of my manuscript, and to whom I would here express my warmest thanks.

PREFACE

This book originated in a larger study of rationalism and its social repercussions, from the Greeks to the present day. However, it soon became plain that the patristic age and the Middle Ages – unlike, say, the Renaissance – do not make sense if viewed predominantly in terms of the legacy of Greek rationalism; since Judaeo-Christian sacralism, in fusion with Hellenic intellectualism, is then the paramount influence. In order to understand the psychic and humane patterns of these periods, which for the most part contradict the teaching of Jesus, and furthermore bear vitally upon the often too glib and unqualified claim that we owe our humanitarianism to Christianity, and also in order to avoid ascribing too much to the Greeks, another dimension of explanation is required. For this we need to explore critically the nature and effects, the true logic and dynamic, of the idea of the Holy, as they present themselves in the Old Testament. The course of this investigation led me, as will be seen, to an interpretation of holiness very different from the traditional one, and much less favourable. But what follows is not a Marxist analysis of religion.

I have thought it best not to extend further the time-span of the present study. After the Middle Ages, sacralism becomes not only a less dominant but a much more diluted phenomenon, whose character and fruits accordingly elude clear identification. It is during those centuries when it held full sway that we can best gauge its psychological and moral consequences, and that an understanding of these is historically most helpful. Furthermore, other intellectual movements, such as the essentially Hellenic and poetic

The Idea of Holiness and the Humane Response

rationalism of the Renaissance, or the reactive prosaic one of the eighteenth century, come to command the scene, at the expense of sacralism. These later periods and their humane responses I discuss, mainly under the aspect of rationalism and the Greek inheritance, in a forthcoming study.

J.H.S. ARMSTRONG

CONTENTS

ACKNOWLEDGEMENTS   vii
PREFACE   ix

PART ONE : THE IDEA OF HOLINESS

1 THE SACRALISM OF THE HEBREWS   3
2 THE HEBREW ATTITUDE TO ANIMALS   34
3 THE POETIC FORMS OF THE HEBREWS   48
4 HEBREW SACRALISM AND THE HUMANE RESPONSE   60
5 HEBREW SACRALISM AND FOREIGN NATIONS   76

PART TWO : THE HISTORIC SEQUEL

6 HOLINESS AND THE HUMANE RESPONSE
   IN THE AGE OF THE FATHERS – I   99
7 HOLINESS AND THE HUMANE RESPONSE
   IN THE AGE OF THE FATHERS – II   119
8 HOLINESS AND THE HUMANE RESPONSE
   IN THE MIDDLE AGES – I   129
9 HOLINESS AND THE HUMANE RESPONSE
   IN THE MIDDLE AGES – II   151

REFERENCES   167

PART ONE

THE IDEA OF HOLINESS

1

THE SACRALISM OF
THE HEBREWS

We begin this study of the cult and worship of the Holy, and its profound consequences for European social history, by considering the outlook of the Hebrews, who bequeathed this religious phenomenon to the West. While Hebrew sacralism is of much interest in itself, and lies at the centre of Judaeo-Christian thought, I believe that it is also impossible to understand the baffling predominant inhumanity of the patristic age and the Middle Ages, and thus in turn to view aright the Christian humanitarian contribution, without first reflecting upon the nature and effects of the concept of holiness, as they reveal themselves in the Old Testament. Our examination of the Hebrew viewpoint will start by exploring what seems to me one of its most fundamental features, namely the deep and insuperable contradiction between two of its principal notions, the concept of holiness and that of the blessing.

1

There runs through the literature of the Hebrews, but particularly its earliest layer, a persistent strand of organic thinking and values, some of whose expressions we shall consider at a later stage. Our immediate concern is with the richest and most original fruit, in Old Testament times, of this side of the Hebrew mind: the idea of the blessing, a concept that dominates the patriarchal legends, but which is also unfolded by sympathetic later thinking. The blessing is at once a being's power to bring to full fruition its unique living totality, and the happiness, the fulfilment and the richness of life, that flow from realising this most fortunate potential. It is epitomised in the simple command 'Be fruitful'; the sense of its infinitely precious quality is distilled when Jacob declares to the angel, with all the tenacious passion of his soul, 'I will not let thee go except thou bless me'; while its common and universal quality is expressed in its being enjoyed by the beasts also, and eventually in the belief that God blessed not only man but every creature under heaven. By natural extension, the blessing radiates to embrace all humankind, for it is promised to Abraham that 'in thee shall all the families of the earth be blessed' – even if there is here an ominous suggestion of a one-way process. God's concern with blessing other peoples is also shown when he protects Hagar and her son Ishmael, and promises to multiply their seed exceedingly, namely their descendants the Bedouin.[1] Even plants are blessed, and in Isaiah it is declared of the grape, 'Destroy it not, for a blessing is in it.'[2]

The idea of the blessing is of course closely bound up with fertility and abundance of posterity, in man and beast, but even here is by no means reducible to these, since the urge to reproduce is inseparable from the complex imaginative and emotional aspirations associated with it. The blessing also operates through the full and free functioning of the whole psyche, the collaboration of its centre and periphery and all that lies between, and through every bridge and encounter by which this state is strengthened and enlarged: man's bond with his forebears, with his cultural origins and his own past, his relationship with his family and intimates and people, his nearness to the beasts of the field. With severe imaginative logic, the patriarchal Hebrew father seeks to pass on to his son (but not unfortunately his daughter) such blessedness as he has accumulated, by blessing him. The blessing works through mutuality and connection, not isolation; through what is shared as a common birthright by all, not what is the preserve of a select few; by addition, not subtraction. It is also inseparable from peace and a cherishing of peace, that good state being necessary for its thriving, as well as enhancing it through harmony with other peoples. Its inner kernel is soundness of being (*tom*), while its riches are seen as an overflowing imaginative and emotional fullness of life, 'largeness of heart, even as the sand that is on the seashore'.[3] The idea of the blessing sets forth a profound and endlessly fruitful truth. It is I believe, in the Old Testament period, by far the most fertile and helpful creation of the Hebrew mind.* And yet alas, it was not destined long to flourish there.

2

For the Hebrew mind was also drawn to, and soon overwhelmingly preferred, a contrary form of mental organisation to that organic one expressed by the blessing, namely a psychic centralism of the most pure and uncompromising kind, whose nature and purpose I shall discuss presently. Accordingly, with the advent early in Hebrew history of Yahwism – which the Israelite group in Egypt most probably took over from the Midianites living east of the Gulf of Aqabah, and subsequently spread to the other Israelite tribes engaged in the occupation of Palestine[4] – the organic and psychologically democratic idea of the blessing came increasingly to be overshadowed by a theoretically allied but fundamentally alien and opposed conception: that of the Holy, a

* For a full discussion of the blessing, see J. Pederson, *Israel*, 1926, vol. 1, ch. 2, 'The Blessing'. As most students in this area must be, I am indebted to Pedersen's fine and penetrating study. But I reach very different conclusions, as will be seen, particularly as regards the compatibility of the concepts of blessing and holiness, and the primacy of historical developments in determining Israel's religious evolution.

word which most significantly does not occur in the patriarchal narratives. Believed to be a consummation of the blessing, a raising of it to its highest pitch, as well as a re-creative influence upon it, in reality it is its denial and antithesis. For the ideal of holiness is the reverse of that of wholeness, the essence of the blessing. Holiness is before all else a sovereign power, which has no need to consult other powers in man, or lowlier creatures and natural forms, and one located in a special centre. The basic principle of holiness is divorce from ordinary human nature and ordinary life. From the first, the heightened psychic strength which it denotes is the prerogative of heroic and pre-eminent supermen – the mighty warrior, the great chieftain, the prophet and priest – and that typically in brief visitations of quite exceptional forcefulness, radically discontinuous with their normal performance, and associated with ritual isolation from everyday life. Even the formidable holy might of these chosen few pales in comparison with that of a central sacred treasure, the ark of the covenant. Holiness must not be weakened by association with ordinary existence, still less contaminated by contact with the unclean, which is finally construed with the utmost high-minded fastidiousness and scrupulosity. It is renewed not from nature's infinity of bountiful sources, but from the utterly isolated and special place, or stone or mountain-top, where it is felt to be uniquely concentrated. Nor does it draw strength from the great republic of ordinary days, with their common pursuits and satisfactions, but from a day of days when these must be suspended, lest they should defile it. It is of the essence of holy bread that it should be unlike profane daily bread.

Always the movement is towards a more severe and dominant cult of holiness, based upon ever more rigorous concentration and exclusion. From a position of there being many sanctuaries in Palestine, cultic centralisation leads to the singling out of one isolated sanctuary, namely the Temple at Jerusalem, as the unique dwelling-place of Yahweh's holy name. Even within that one sanctified domain, the holy area steadily contracts. At first, the altar in the open hall is a focus of holiness, as well as the inner temple cell, and the ordinary people could apparently gather there round it. But eventually the inner cell, the Holy of Holies, acquires a monopoly of holiness, and takes on such concentrated holy power that the people may not even approach its outlying hall. Only one select member of a sacerdotal class, namely the high priest, is now holy enough to enter the Holy of Holies, and that only once a year. Above all, the cult of the holy is consummated in the ever more awful isolation and incomparability of Israel's god, the centre and one true focus of holiness. 'Who is like thee, the proven powerful by holiness, terrible in glorious deeds, doing wonders?'[5] 'There is none holy like Yahweh.'[6] 'Holy, Holy, Holy is Yahweh of hosts.'[7] 'Who is able to stand before Yahweh, this holy god?'[8] Before such an apotheosis of holiness, the only proper human reaction is to shrink in awe and dread. Now all these concentrations of power and significance, in special and isolated centres, serve, I believe, one formative psychological aim: they express and strengthen and justify movement towards a particular form of mental organisation, the unalleviatedly centralised. By this I mean a pure and absolute psychic centralism, as opposed to a system where the centre is needfully pre-eminent but does not isolate itself and assume autocratic control, because it remains in consultative union with the human totality. From the beginning, holiness signified and was harnessed to producing a high-pitched intensity of inner strength, generated by the total, rather than qualified ascendancy of a psychic dominant, which in the case of the Hebrews was what Milton calls 'the unconquerable Will'; whose despotic rule and maximal force the cult of the Holy served to establish.

3

In order to understand this centralist essential function of sacralism, and also to see what aims this function finally served, we next turn to the heart and essence of holiness, the holy god of Israel. The psychic and cultural importance of such exalted deities hardly needs stressing. But something must first be said of their primary purpose, and of some important differences of type. The growing psychic central-ism *to some extent* needful to a would-be civilised culture tends to support itself, I believe, particularly in its vulnerable early stages, by imagining loftily sited divinities made in man's ideal image of himself, and living his own life in just the form brought about by the new psychological order, but in incredibly privileged circumstances; who glorify the emergent centralist regime and lend it cosmic validation; sanctify its principle of betterment from what is high; and nurture it through communing with great residents of the mind, who are really enlarged projections of itself and its aims.

Sometimes, the uplifting and humanisation of deities is accompanied by crucial checks and controls, so that the psychic centre is not disastrously over-fortified, with the result that it becomes an isolated inner autocrat which does not consult the human whole it should serve. At this point, I think it will be helpful to pause momentarily to consider a particularly revealing instance of such qualifications: those introduced by men whom we are apt mistakenly to think too remote in time for real relevance or interest, namely the Sumerians, that deeply imaginative ancient people whose great civilisation flourished in the delta of the Tigris and Euphrates during the third millennium BC. Not only did the Sumerians invent and develop one of the first effective sys-tems of writing, leave us the first substantial literature we possess, whose humane amplitude still has power to move, produce sculptures which stand comparison with those of any age, and create a body of primary myth which greatly influenced Hebrew mythology, and probably the Greek likewise.[9] They are also notable for the incipiently human-itarian social reforms of some of their rulers, reforms of which I shall say a little more later, but even more so for certain proverbs (likewise briefly considered in due course) which show a pained and immediate awareness of the *concrete miseries* of poverty, the kernel of true and effective humanitarianism. Although our bias against the very old and unfamiliar may tell us otherwise, the Sumerians can teach us much.

For the Sumerians made a profoundly creative assault upon one of the main problems of civilised life: how to embrace the greater centralism necessary for civilised achievement, yet keep it subservient to the human totality and its needs. The stubbornly organic outlook of the Sumerians – which though early is not primitive, since it survives into a complex civilisation, and has affinities here in modern times, for instance with the Dutch retention of organic values, in combination with advance to civilised achievement – would not allow them blindly to seek ever more absolute centralism, in whatever cause, to risk carrying it far beyond what is humanly contributive. In the field of humane self-awareness, the Sumerians seem thus to have understood certain fundamentals, vital to happiness and fulfilment, which history shows it is all too easy to get wrong, so that men build majestic but finally unhelpful edifices of thought upon mistaken axioms. And nowhere is this plainer than in the Sumerian approach to the sophistic-ation of religion. For, as well as preserving their integrity by tenaciously maintaining connection with the beasts, the Sumerians also did so through carefully avoiding too drastic a separation of their newly elevated and humanised deities from the natural world, by still representing them as the inner and sustaining principles of living forms which they originally were.

In the beginning, the divine was seemingly for the Sumerian not something transcendent and distinct from animal or tree or plant but what Thorkild Jacobsen well calls 'power at the centre of its being, the vital force causing it to be and making it thrive and flourish'.[10] Thus it comes about, for example, that the Sumerian word *ezinnu* denotes alike the corn goddess, the grain dropped in the earth, and the green stalks 'standing in the furrow like a lovely young girl'. The names of certain other Sumerian gods and goddesses are likewise identical with those of natural phenomena. This early phase of Sumerian religious feeling is not something essentially obscure or remote from us. It simply voices, in a language we can still well understand, that within us which continually warms and stands amazed at the fullness of nature, how surely and with what marvellous precision her processes and forms satisfy our psychic needs, even as they provide for our physical; which makes it entirely natural to think and speak here of divinities, even if our own intellectual sophistication will not allow this; and which indicates their siting precisely where the awed reaction originates, at the mysterious heart of living structures.

Probably during the third millennium BC, and incipiently as early as the fourth, the Sumerians elevated and humanised their gods, turning them into a magnified landed aristocracy, inhabiting high heaven in ideal circumstances. But this is by no means the whole story. For the Sumerians were deeply reluctant to remove their deities from those vital structures of which they had once been conceived to be the life-giving inner principles. Accordingly, even after exalting them and endowing them with human form, they continued to envisage them in the old role. From the body of the corn goddess there still springs the actual and living grain. The valiant Utu (the sun god) is also 'the firm standing bull'. Ningizzida, the divine intermediary, 'lord of the good tree', does not cease sometimes to be presented *as the trunk of a tree*. The love and fertility goddess Inanna, later the Babylonian Ishtar, claiming that she is 'greater than the other gods', boasts that she is 'a wild cow leading the way'. Ishkar is at once the weather god and the south wind. As Jacobsen justly observes, 'To the latest time, the older forms retain a curious vitality, seeming to lurk under the human exterior ready to break through it to reveal the true essence of the divine power and will.'[11] The remote exaltation and the humanised character of the new Sumerian pantheon were thus greatly qualified, and its disconnection from nature averted. The psychic importance of such anchors to windward would be hard to exaggerate. When the sophistication of religion is limited in this way, the centre tends not to be excessively strengthened, and to stay in consultative union with the human totality. When later we briefly compare the Hebrew humane response with the Sumerian, we shall see that the Sumerians did not lose in moral stature from this arrangement of their mental life, or the religion falling short of final loftiness that shaped it, but rather the reverse.

But, more typically, a centralising culture hurls itself with little check or reserve upon an elevated and humanised religion, with the result that the over-supported centre aggrandises itself into despotic dominance. Infatuated with centralist holiness, the Hebrews embraced, with all the fiery fervour of their nature and temperament, the latter course. They did so even more uncompromisingly than the Greeks. For the Greeks, who desired a varied play of the higher faculties, leading to many-sided excellence (including success in war but by no means confined to this), and based upon the ascendancy of reason, chose appropriately to express and strengthen their emergent centralism through a divine oligarchy, an Olympian aristocratic society ever more dominated by a central Zeus - yet one that also accommodated to some extent the irrational in themselves, by including correspondent deities, such as Aphrodite and Dionysus. But the controlling aspirations of the Hebrews were very different from those of the Greeks, and so they had to create correspondingly different divine support.

4

The Hebrews overwhelmingly sought sheer psychic strength and potency, yielding the martial prowess necessary for the gaining of land and political status. For they soon emerge as a people dominated by consuming territorial and self-aggrandising ambition, having origins perhaps in lack of soil of their own and the wounds of servitude, who are empowered to win territory through conquest and eviction, by a national god whose main role is to confer land and greatness. 'Unto thy seed have I given this land, from the river of Egypt unto the great river, the river Euphrates: the Kenites, and the Kenizzites, and the Kadmonites, and the Hittites, and the Perrizites, and the Rephaims, and the Amorites, and the Canaanites, and the Girgashites, and the Jebusites.'[12] 'I will make of thee a great nation . . . make thy name great.'* In the words of David's hymn of thanksgiving to Yahweh, 'Thou hast made me the head of the heathen: a people which I knew not shall serve me'.[13] 'Ask of me, and I shall give thee the heathen for thine inheritance, and the uttermost parts of the earth for thy possession.'[14] Yahweh is the one who 'smote great nations and slew mighty kings . . . and *gave their land* for an heritage, an heritage unto Israel his servant'.[15] The theme of land – the seizing of it by the power of Israel's god, its loss due to sin, and its restoration through a penitent waiting upon Yahweh – is a leitmotiv, if not the principal one, in the Old Testament. Throughout this literature, the incomparability of Yahweh is closely connected with his feats of war, his supposed historic interventions to give victory to the Hebrews in their drive to occupy land (and to make possible the exodus from Egypt which unleashes it), doing for his people great and terrible things. We need to separate this harsh reality from the fervent

---

* Gen. 12, 2. We should remember here that this section of Genesis is full of interpolations – sometimes obvious, at others not reliably separable from ancient tradition – by the Yahwist and Elohist collectors, interpreting the patriarchal experience and destiny from the standpoint of Mosaic Yahwism.

poetry, and high conceptual rigmarole, of a chosen people, covenant and promise, redemption and saving acts, in which Hebrew writers lovingly wrap it. Biblical theologians have, I believe, tended to treat these resonant justificatory notions much too uncritically, taking them at their creators' own valuation, and ignoring the hard fact of successful aggression which they obscure. Seeking a pure and undifferentiated centralism then, giving the concentrated psychic intensity and purposefulness needed to fulfil their territorial obsession, the Hebrews opted for a single god who would not brook even subordinated peers. Consequently, we shall find that monolithic Hebrew sacralism had power, when superadded through the eventual union of Judaism and Hellenism, to purify the already severe centralism of the Greeks, eliminating such inadequate, yet crucially helpful, space as it made for non-rational elements, and importing a new dimension of rigidity and fanaticism.

Nevertheless, the similarity between the Hebrew and Greek forms of centralism, and so between their respective supporting deities, is sufficiently close to give rise to revealing parallels. Both psychic systems, being each embraced as giving the power to excel in one form or another, lead to cults of excellence, with their characteristic craving for glory and honour, fierce hostility to all rivals, and typical luminous imagery.* In Israel's god, this takes the form of rabid jealousy for his incomparable glory, expressed in many a boasting of unique magnificence, but definitively when he proclaims, 'I am Yahweh, that is my name, and my glory I give not to another.'[16] Accordingly, he is styled the 'God of Glory' and the 'King of Glory', and the psalmist sings of his 'glorious honour'.[17] The supreme 'honour' of Yahweh is a recurrent theme in the Psalms. A Hebrew warrior-hero is expected to display the same dazzling radiance as the Greek, to 'be as the sun when he goeth forth in his might',[18] and to achieve the same blaze of glory: the acme of success is to

* I discuss the Greek cult of excellence more fully in my forthcoming study, Poetic Rationalism and the Renaissance.

'inherit the throne of glory'.[19] The imagery here has much the same battering brightness as that which surrounds the excelling Homeric hero, who is also set before us as a figure overpoweringly effulgent, sometimes in like astral terms:

> She kindled from his helm and shield flame unwearying, like to the star of harvest that shines bright above all others, when he hath bathed him in the stream of Ocean.[20]

The Israelite king, who enjoys a unique link with the national deity, is the focus of correspondingly unbridled dreams of pre-eminence:

> He shall have dominion also from sea to sea, and from the river unto the ends of the earth . . . Yea, all kings shall fall down before him: all nations shall serve him.[21]

This is language fundamentally similar to that of Agamemnon and Achilles, with their honorific obsession, resolved so to excel that men will shrink to speak of themselves as their equals, but carried to an even more extreme pitch. There is an important difference, however, between the Hebrew cult of excellence and the Greek. Among the Greeks, the main craving for glory was individual. With the Hebrews, on the other hand, it was primarily communal, despite the heroisation of particular warriors and kings, while true glory was reserved for the national deity. Thus, whereas the Greek cult of excellence was socially divisive, as we are reminded by the quarrel at the centre of the *Iliad*, that of the Hebrews mainly was not.

Similarly, both Hebrew sacralist centralism and Greek rationalism lead to an imperious and administrative distancing of nature, through a subordination of her to man-made preconceptions and designs. Whereas the Greeks over-ridingly see nature as demonstrating the omnipresence of

reason, and gratifying everywhere a rationalistic aesthet-
icism, for the Hebrews she comes to proclaim the splendour
and dominion of centralised power, as represented by
Israel's god, and to be a storehouse of symbolism serving to
convey it, a view of the natural world which we shall consider later. Both approaches, while producing much invocation and praise of nature, end in alienation from her, by
working against an experiencing and humbly consultative
response. Finally, both centralist psychologies generate the
idea of the terrible transgression, which enlarges and justifies
a punitive supreme deity: the Hebrew, the idea of sin, to
which we shall return; and the Greek, that of the fatal
hubristic offence. Moreover, each of these notions is associated with a doctrine of inherited guilt, whereby the
innocent descendants of offenders make divine justice more
fearful, and so the god who administers it greater and more
terrible, through being held to qualify for punishment, and
abundantly receiving it. No wonder, therefore, that Judaism
and Hellenism, being for all their notable differences
primarily cognate and compatible, eventually combined in a
fusion of Hebrew and Hellenic thought, but above all in a
mutually supportive ascendancy over the Western mind.

5

The evolution of Israel's holy god immeasurably assists
Hebrew movement towards pure centralism and enjoyment
of its territorial rewards. For he becomes a deity ever more
uplifted and remote, increasingly thought of in terms of
holiness as absolute centralised power, whose main function
is to support and enforce the emergent psychology which
fashions him, so furthering its aims. The god of the Hebrews
is always in principle monistic, the one sustainer of his clan
or people; although originally each of the three main patri-
archs, Abraham, Isaac and Jacob – in all likelihood founders
of separate cults, and not yet in the lineal relationship of

later tradition – probably had different such nameless gods who were later united through the rise to supremacy of the Mosaic Yahweh.[22] But at first he is a present and closely accompanying god, whose proximity is distilled in the simple phrase 'I will be with thee'. At the same time, he is specially to be met in a variety of sacred places, if in ominously few. His principal function is to give and renew the blessing, a role fulfilled by constant life-giving activity, while he also protects and guides the nomadic herdsman as he travels, and strengthens his hope of eventually gaining land of his own. He is likewise a benignly nebulous being, who can readily be imagined as permeating the life of man and beast – in brief, a credible giver of blessing.

With the advent of Mosaic Yahwism, however, Israel's god begins to withdraw into awesome elevation, at length becoming uplifted immeasurably far above the human and natural spheres. Yahweh who 'dwelleth on high' is one who 'humbleth himself to behold the things that are in heaven, and in the earth'.[23] No longer is he now primarily a giver of blessing, although theoretically he still retains this attribute, but rather overwhelmingly the sole real centre of holiness seen as absolute centralised power, a deity only really suited to show forth unimaginable strength, to hold the reins of the universe and inhabit eternity, to vanquish all rivals and enable his favoured few to do the same, but with no diminishing reliance upon their martial resources. Appropriately, he takes on a new ethnic exclusiveness: no longer content with the fruitful but intangible activity of blessing, he increasingly prefers the barren yet unmistakably potent one of exalting one race over all the world. Consequently, his warlike character and warrior attributes are ever more stressed: he is a 'dread warrior',[24] bares and wields his 'mighty arm', triumphs gloriously over his enemies. More and more, he comes to resemble an expansionist and always victorious despotic monarch. Pursuing the same drive to aggrandisement, at first he is simply mightier than other gods, then their king and judge, and finally the only god.

And he is conceived solely as having human shape, albeit of a most exalted kind not to be represented in visible form, never like the Sumerian gods as an animal or tree. As Pedersen well observes,

> David's Yahweh is so personal that he stands apart from the life of man and nature. His influence in nature and in man does not become weaker on that account, quite the contrary. But he cannot be merged with other souls, he is self-contained and acts from afar. The soul of animals and plants has no part in his nature, the character of his soul is throughout like that of a man. He demands honour and more honour as an Israelitish ruler. He is almost an Israelite among other Israelites, only he is so mighty that all must give way to him.[25]

In other words, Israel's god becomes an ideal Israelite of the new psychic persuasion, realising the latter's chosen centralism, and the aggrandisement through potency which it yields, on an unimaginably splendid scale. This inexorable promotion of the god of Israel, into a perfect image of emergent Hebrew pyschology and its proper ambitions, is consummated in two linked doctrines: belief in Yahweh as creator of the world and the conception of him as ruler of history.

6

Israel's god progressively withdraws from the natural world, to become its lofty creator, controlling the forms and forces of nature which he has made, but present in none. Partly, the inbuilt logic of a centralist and holy deity demanded that he should thus extricate himself from nature and be primarily its architect. Yahweh was almost bound eventually to become the performer of one transcendent act of cosmic creation, as the proper consummation of his sacralist character. For to create the universe is the most dramatic and conclusive exhibition of centralised power that can readily be imagined, while it also saves him from diffuse immersion in living forms and processes, which detracts from pure centrality. But the needs of territorially advantageous potency, which seems to be the main object of Hebrew sacralism, pressed even more strongly in this direction. Yahweh can only give his people a territorially preferential position – or rather confer the ultimate certainty and purposefulness which they need to win this for themselves, particularly since they are a small nation surrounded by larger hostile powers – if he is believed to be able and entitled to dispose of the world as he likes; and the best way to that felt ability and right is to be held to be the maker of the world. At the same time, it is the trump card that disposes of the claims, and so the daunting power, of other national gods: 'for all the gods of the nations are idols, but the Lord made the Heavens'.[26] In other words, belief in Yahweh's status as creator completes his power to enhance Hebrew forcefulness, by giving total confidence that he can, both rightly and inexorably, confer historic superiority in terms of the conquest of land. That he should be thought also to control world events consummates his effectiveness in this role. Accordingly, the growth of belief in Yahweh as creator and the growth of belief in him as ruler of history are parallel and inseparable developments.

There is no significant evidence that the original patriarchal concept of deity involved the idea of cosmic creator.[27] The claim that Yahweh was cosmic creator apparently first comes at the beginning of the sixth century, when Jeremiah attributes to him the words 'I made the earth with my great strength and with outstretched arm, I made man and beast on the face of the earth'. The cosmic creation story at the beginning of Genesis[28] is considerably later, belonging to its latest stratum, the Priestly Document ('P'), whose composition

(c. 538–450) falls in the post-exilic period.* The prophet most concerned to establish Yahweh's power of cosmic creation is, of course, Deutero-Isaiah of the Exile,[29] whose activity belongs to the period 587–530. From the first, the emergent conception of Yahweh as creator is largely urged into being by his function of conferring territorial gain and greatness. Even in the early traditions of the Bible, almost certainly before Yahweh is thought of as having created the world, he is forced to become incipiently its master by his role of supposedly intervening on Israel's behalf, to assist her irresistible march to conquer and annex the promised land, and maintain her occupation of it. He divides the Red Sea, nourishes his people with manna, and gives them water from the rock. He destroys great numbers of the opposing Amorites with hailstones, and sends his thunder against the Philistines.[30] When he marches out to war against the Canaanites, the earth trembles, the heavens drop, the clouds drop water.[31] And the developed doctrine of Yahweh as creator, as set forth by Jeremiah and Deutero-Isaiah, is still harnessed to his purpose of providing territorial possession; for his status as creator gives him the right to bestow land as he sees fit. The words of Jeremiah just quoted, asserting that God made the earth, are followed immediately by the claim, 'I give it to whomsoever it seems fit to me'. Again, when Deutero-Isaiah prophesies that Yahweh will send Cyrus the Persian to conquer the Babylonian oppressors and restore the Israelites in triumph to their rightful land, he sees the god's ability to do so as stemming from his might as creator, and as the essential significance of that power and status:

---

* See Fohrer, op. cit., p. 179. For the three narrative sources in Genesis, see Gerhard von Rad, *Das erste Buch Mose, Genesis,* 1956, tr. John H. Marks, 1961, pp. 23–30. The creation story in Gen. 2, 4b–25 is considerably earlier, belonging to the Yahwistic source stratum in Genesis (c. 950), the earliest in the book, but speaks only of the creation of man (*adam*), and not of the creation of heaven and earth.

I alone, I made the earth and created man upon it.
I with my own hands stretched out the heavens and
all their host. I alone have aroused this man in
righteousness: he shall build my city, he shall restore
my captives . . .[32]

There is a difference between Jeremiah and Deutero-Isaiah as
to how Yahweh, creator of the world, will bestow his territorial favours. Jeremiah is reconciled to impending
Babylonian supremacy, as a judgement upon Judah for her
sins. Deutero-Isaiah, as has just been said, foresees that
Yahweh will use his cosmic power directly on behalf of
Israel. But the territorial thrust of belief in Yahweh as
creator is the same in both. In the psalmist's vision, it is the
god who 'made the heavens' and 'stretched out the earth'
who is proclaimed in the same breath to be the one who
'overthrew Pharaoh and his host', 'smote great nations and
slew mighty kings', and gave their land as 'an heritage unto
Israel his servant'.[33] The demands then of centralist
sacralism, but still more of its territorial and aggrandising
objective, required and ensured Yahweh's simultaneous
promotion to cosmic creator and ruler of history; although
the intolerable rival claims of the Babylonian Marduk
apparently spurred the Hebrews into finalising their own
god's long-evolving ones.

The religious evolution just reviewed is ascribed by
Pedersen to historic factors, namely the rise of the monarchy
and the humiliating experience of exile, the one calling for a
concentration of divinity uniquely mediated by the king,
which in turn required him to become creator of the earth,
the other demanding a compensative elevation of Israel's god
over all the world. Now I have no wish to deny that Israel's
religious evolution is rooted in its history. But, while these
historic developments may well have been important precipitants, as fundamental explanations they do not, I think,
convince. Surely, they could only have unleashed such
momentous change, especially in a people so notably able to

retain whatever it passionately wants to retain, by furthering and riding an already present psychic current of great power. These alterations in the character of Israel's god were rather psychologically inevitable almost from the beginning, written into the Hebrews' soon-embraced new psychic priorities. It is the inner logic of these preferred aspirations, the pursuit of centralist holiness in the interest of conquest and aggrandisement, that in due time required and called forth a heavenly vindicator, a vast image of their emergent psychology and its objectives, in the most consummated imaginable form, the Holy One of Israel. That huge and awesome Hebrew image eventually joined with fundamentally like productions of the Greek mind to impose upon European culture these peoples' basically similar mental regime.

We shall see in a moment that this uncompromising elevation of their national deity created great problems for the Hebrews. For while blessing was still attributed to him, in strict subordination to the conferring of territorial advantage, he was no longer a coherent or finally credible giver of it, that being the natural role of a god or gods still in vital and intimate connection with man and nature. This left the Hebrews wide open to the appeal of other gods, who had kept near to, and involved with, the natural order, in particular the fertility gods of the Canaanites. The advance of Israel's god to transcendent centrality is not, of course, the whole story. We must shortly consider attempts by certain prophets to qualify the sacralist idea of the remote Holy One, by including vitally connective but finally incompatible aspects, derived from the organic part of their inheritance. But modification, through benign compensative elements at odds with its dominant character, was not enough, even if it had been able to win general acceptance. Nothing less than reconstruction from the ground floor up would genuinely have reformed the conception, making it other than essentially opposed to the organic notion of the blessing, and altering the centralist thrust which made all but inevitable its eventual alliance with Greek rationalism. Unfortunately, it was much too strongly formulated and firmly established for that.

7

Finally, the rise of the centralist cult of holiness and of the Holy One was greatly assisted by the growth of an ancillary conception, the profoundly anti-organic notion of sin, a word which tolls through Hebrew literature ever more insistently and with ever more sombre overtones. Hebrew thought increasingly views human life as pervaded and threatened by sin, a chronic state of rebellion against God, uncleanness of heart, but above all utter inadequacy before the transcendent majesty of divine holiness. Indeed, a large part of the mission of the prophets is to strengthen and deepen this conviction. The main social effect of belief in sin is to create a 'guilt culture', that is to say one which sees man as quite unfit to stand in any boldness before his heavenly overlord or overlords, as finding his proper place in the dust of self-abasement, and as a rightful object of denunciatory and retributive divine anger. It is one which contrasts sharply with the 'shame culture' of the Sumerians, whose gods and goddesses are fundamentally uncensorious, being represented as loving virtue in man yet paradoxically as also finally responsible for some of his forms of immoral conduct, and witholding immortality from man not as retribution for his sin but because they are determined to keep the best things for themselves, just as they send the Flood not in order to denounce man's wickedness but because their human underlings are multiplying too fast and becoming a nuisance to them. Our present concern is with the force and darkness of the conception of sin, not with its minute history, and of these we are sufficiently reminded by Yahweh's fearful condemnation of human sinfulness before sending the Flood, 'And God saw that the wickedness of man was great in the earth, and that every imagination of the thoughts of his heart was only evil continually',[34] by the psalmist's terrible self-accusation, 'Behold, I was shapen in iniquity; and in sin did my mother conceive me',[35] and perhaps most of all by his simple words, 'My sin is ever before me'.[36] The authority and size of the idea are magnified by the great drama of sin and atonement that runs through the Bible, by the belief that man and nature continue to suffer because of Adam's sin of disobedience, and by the whole system of sacrificial ceremonies and purificatory rites through which the conviction of sin is relieved and the favour and mercy of Yahweh hopefully regained. There is no need to rehearse further how pervasive in the Old Testament is the idea of sin, when the reader, if he wants to enlarge the picture, can so easily do this for himself.[37]

The notion of sin seems to me not only one of the most powerful but also one of the darkest and most unhelpful ever devised by the human mind. For our human integrity prompts us to think of its frequent disruptions, losses of vital connection within and without, as arising from omissions or mistakes, and possibly tragic ones, but not from sin; although it sometimes needs to invoke the blunt instrument of blame and condemnation, the strong and unmistakable labels 'right' and 'wrong', or even the still stronger one of 'evil'. The fundamental reason for this, surely, is that the ideas of neglect and error imply, as that of sin does not, a right and helpful trust in the basically unimpaired collaborative soundness and resilience of the human organism, its tenacious ability to pick itself up, find the right path again and continue its journey, perhaps even enhancing its understanding and richness of life by learning from its mistakes. But sin, which denotes an offence against holiness, is a word with overwhelmingly self-mistrustful, self-condemnatory and pessimistic implications, as well as profoundly centralist ones. It signifies a catastrophic defilement and betrayal of a psychic centre which ought to be perfect, because sovereign in virtue of unique fitness to be holy and acceptable to the Holy One; so that the least transgression against holiness fatally breaches this mandatory perfection, thus denaturing and incapacitating the all-important central point of control. And this leads us to view ourselves, with quite unrealistic and most destructive fear and self-denigration, as flawed and guilty souls, indeed probably so from our youth up, unfit to continue on life's pilgrimage and even unworthy to tread the earth, without elaborate prostrations and purifications, self-searchings and reproachings, which in turn strengthen the conviction of sinfulness – in short, as miserable sinners. But, assuredly, the concept of sin encouraged the obsession with holiness, together with awe of the Holy One, and was a main instrument by which these were enforced. Against the rage for holiness, supported by the flight from sin, the idea of the blessing could not prevail. Thus it could only retreat into the background, and sometimes bear rich fruit which proclaims its inextinguishable fertility, and enduring hold upon the Jewish heart.

8

The organic attitude represented by the blessing, as has just been said, was overshadowed but not extinguished by the opposed centralist idea of holiness, contracting into a persistent recessive strand in Hebrew thinking, to fructify in due time. We next turn to the two most notable Old Testament expressions of this endurance of organic responses among the Hebrews, which also illustrate both their incompatibility with sacralist aims and their final inability to prevail against them: namely the thought of Hosea, and of the author of Jonah.

But at this point, when it begins to appear more often, I must first clarify the word 'organic' and also issue a caveat against a misunderstanding that is liable to arise from its use. This word I employ, periodically and with reluctance, as the best way of referring succinctly to a particular psychic stance and set of values, those defined much more precisely by the idea of the blessing and its related imagery. I use 'organic' to denote briefly what can be summarised only in approximate terms: namely a psychic system which ensures that the human vital totality (including, when it becomes more complex, its properly developed higher faculties) fully functions as such, and a cherishing by man of his bond of kinship with the rest of living nature, not only because this is one inevitable and fulfilling outcome of an entire human life but also because it is necessary for its maintenance and renewal. But, although the word 'organic' is a useful means of short-hand reference here, we must be constantly mindful of its inherent inadequacy and power to confuse, both of which it shares with other general terms, when applied in the psychic sphere.

The subtle entirety of an integrated human life, its strange and infinitely delicate interplay of diverse elements, cannot be adequately defined by abstractions and generalities. No doubt it would be most convenient if the right collaboration of our faculties could be precisely identified by a general concept. But, fortunately for the complexity and richness of our existence, we are not made in a way that allows this. Rather, the rightful intricate unity of our life is realised sufficiently only by minutely exact poetic forms – the idea of the blessing, and its associated images being one example – forms which we fatally devalue if we treat them as merely duplicating the products of conceptual thinking, or as just expressing picturesquely what can be conveyed quite efficiently by abstract ideas. By the same token, human integrity is understood by patiently attending to appropriate poetic formations, and to that in man and nature which they alone truly set forth.

As no more than a rough-and-ready label, then, the word 'organic' is needed here if our inquiry is not to lose shape and momentum, through constant rehearsing of poetic material. On the other hand, it is also apt, unless we are continually alert to the danger, to persuade us that we have solved a problem we have scarcely begun to touch. For it can easily seduce us into thinking we can bypass the whole long task of imaginatively exploring human integrity, by creating the illusion that it has rendered this superfluous.

9

I will begin then with Hosea, who taught in northern Israel during the second half of the eighth century. He is a thinker whose stature and originality it would be hard to exaggerate, for he applied himself to the central problem of developed Hebrew religion: its need to bring its god once more into intimate and vital connection with man and his life, having removed him from both, through determination to exalt the Holy One far above all else, setting him beyond the constraints of earthly involvement.

Hosea's immediate problem is the old and persistent one of the mixed worship of Yahweh and the Canaanite Baal, or rather Baals or Baalim, for the name denotes the patron giver of fruitfulness to a particular piece of soil; although these many local gods were also amalgamated into one Baal, preserver of creation and source of all fertility. For Hosea, the worship of Baalim in conjunction with Yahweh is apostasy against him, an adulterous desertion of Israel's one true god for usurpers and detractors. Accordingly, Hosea denounces the faithlessness of the Israelites and the supposedly degraded nature of Baalistic rites, pleads with Israel to remember Yahweh's mighty historic interventions on her behalf and her covenant with him, and threatens misery and destruction if the Hebrews do not abandon foreign customs and return to their own god. But Hosea goes much deeper than this. Not content with the superficial and doubtfully effective solution of denunciation, pleading and threats, he discerns the root of the problem: the Hebrews' lack of close communion with their god, the inevitable price of making

him remote, which has made them susceptible to the immed-
iacies of Baal worship. The elevation of Yahweh beyond the
human and natural spheres had inevitably left a dangerous
vacuum in the whole crucial organic area, all too liable to be
filled by less exalted deities who had kept connection with
it, and to give these gods an overwhelming appeal. In view
of this, no wonder even the notably loyal Hebrews were so
prone to wander after strange gods, and then bitterly
reproach themselves for faithlessness. Hosea perceives this
consequent general separation between his people and their
god. 'My people are destroyed for lack of knowledge'.[38]
There is no 'knowledge of God in the land'.[39] And, intuiting
something of its cause, he essays a remedy, drawing upon
the earlier Hebrew tradition of organic thinking and feeling,
but not disdaining also to borrow Baalistic ideas and
language that accord with it.

For Hosea seeks to reunite the Hebrews with their god, to
restore their immediate sense of him as a giver of blessing,
through a series of tenderly integrative organic images. In
relation to Israel, Yahweh is like the father of a loved child:

When Israel was a child, then I loved him, and called
my son out of Egypt.[40]

The relationship between Yahweh and Israel is like marriage,
a marital bond that she has betrayed by whoredom, but
which will be restored to perpetual bethrothal; however,
Hosea never expressly calls Yahweh Israel's 'husband',
probably because this is one of the meanings of 'Baal', who
was regarded as owner-husband of the land. Israel was once
to Yahweh 'like grapes in the wilderness' or 'like the first fruit
on the fig-tree'. When she returns to him, he will nurture
her as his seed, and infuse her whole life as a blessedly fructi-
fying force:

And I will sow her unto me in the earth.[41]

Or again,

> I will be as the dew unto Israel: he shall grow as the
> lily, and cast forth his roots as Lebanon.[42]

With profound insight, Hosea sees humane behaviour too as
the natural fruit of this god-given fertility:

> Sow to yourself in righteousness, reap in mercy; break
> up your fallow ground: for it is time to seek the Lord,
> till he come and rain righteousness upon you.[43]

For all his searching and creative quality of mind, Hosea was
too pious and conservative a thinker directly to confront the
ideal of holiness, or to explore the implications of his organic
vision's conflict with it. Rather, he makes a token attempt to
square his viewpoint with sacralism, through that most
touchingly contradictory of biblical phrases, 'the Holy One
in the midst of thee'.[44] Yet it is most significant that Hosea
uses it only on this one occasion. Much later, we find in the
poetry of William Blake a broadly similar shrinking from the
centralism and cold remoteness of holiness, combined with
reluctance, due to his singular veneration of the Hebrew
tradition, to dispense with the conception. For instance,
Blake denounces 'The Accuser, Holy God of All', and
speaks of 'the Cruelties of Holiness', and 'the Satanic Body
of Holiness', yet also affirms incongruously, 'For everything
that lives is holy.'[45] There is, however, in Blake more desire
to compromise here than Hosea shows, a heroic yet finally
unviable attempt to have things both ways by adopting a
halfway-house position, to seek to marry the sacralist vision
with the organic, which he largely owed to the eighteenth-
century movement towards organic values. Indeed, there is
in Blake's poetry a moving conflict between his instinctive
anti-sacralism, and his passionate belief in the inspired and
truly poetic quality of Hebrew literature (over against the
Greek, which he denounces as mechanical and uninspired), a

belief which called for retention of the concept of holiness, as being a central one in Hebrew writing. It is these factors which lead him incongruously to blend sacralist and organic images in his best-known poem; to proclaim that the 'Lamb of God' was 'holy', with all the word's connotations of isolation and distance from nature, but walked 'upon England's mountains green', and was seen on her 'pleasant pastures'; and, more poignant still, that Jerusalem, the holy city and a prime symbol of holiness, shall yet be build 'in England's green and pleasant Land'.[46]

But Hosea's benign innovative thought, which seeks to bring God once more near to man, could not prevail, and for a simple reason. The attempt to qualify the holiness of Yahweh by ascribing to him organic attributes, such as father or husband, or the dew of blessing, embodies an incoherence and confusion: the idea that we can fully register a god as at once remote and near, holy and organically connected, exalted far above all that is in the earth and vitally related to it, the unimaginable monarch of the Universe, and in primary biological relationship with man and beast. For these ways of thinking pull in opposite directions. Moving either way means withdrawing to some extent from the other. Full consummation of either viewpoint entails jettisoning its contrary. We can of course imagine a deity *half-heartedly* or alternately under these opposed aspects, so firmly believing in both, having a foot in the mental world of each, and maintaining them in some sort of tension, but without reaching a coherent viewpoint. Likewise, we can temporise, by adopting halfway-house images which combine both aspects in reduced form, usually with a bias in one direction or the other, thus blurring without removing their final incompatibility. Such an image is the organically-inclined one of God as shepherd, which takes away his monarchical aspect and gives proximity and biological engagement, yet also distances him through separation of form and greater stature, mastery and incomparably superior intelligence. We can too, if we want, proclaim an impossible feat of contradictory thinking and feeling to be possible, through a mysterious compatibility of what conflicts, for instance by juggling with theological terms and conceptions more manipulable than human nature, such as transcendence and immanence. The history of thought is full of such poignant woolly compromises, whereby men who desperately want to have something both ways persuade themselves that it can be done. And the impossibility of giving a full and simultaneous welcome to sacralist and organic images is rooted in a more fundamental one, namely that of wholly embracing two opposed psychologies at the same time. In the last analysis, it is because we cannot adopt both a purely centralist and an integrative psychological system that we cannot reconcile, or completely accept the expressive and enforcing symbols of both.

Thus imaginatively severe and passionate men must choose, giving their main and determinative allegiance to one form of mental organisation or the other, that which seems to them the most true and satisfying, and to one set of images rather than the other. The Hebrew mind in general, being nothing if not severe and passionate, was bound to choose the Holy and its proper symbolism, having opted long before to give this conception overriding priority. By the same token, it had to reject the organic direction and language offered by Hosea, never building upon it and at most making rare use of it, which it duly did. Later Old Testament prophets do not significantly develop, or even draw upon extensively, his images which vitally connect God with man.

10

Lastly, the durability and richness of the organic strand in Hebrew thought, and its final ineffectuality too, are no less clearly seen in that small post-exilic masterpiece, the Book of Jonah. Its author is the one Old Testament prophet (except perhaps to a lesser extent the author of Ruth, about which I shall say a little more later) who may truly be called a follower of Hosea, in the sense of drawing in a like sustained way upon a profound feeling for the organic strand in Hebrew thought; although we do not know how much he is indebted to his predecessor, and how much simply to the same tradition of thinking. He is also a thinker hardly less searching than Hosea, since he concerns himself with the most disturbing moral consequence of sacralism, presently to be considered: namely a raging will to annihilate the unholy, as an intolerable exception and threat to the pure ascendancy of holiness. The Book of Jonah is a cry of protest against this last merciless but logical compulsion, from out the heart of the old organic viewpoint. Accordantly, its author never once uses the word 'holy', or 'holiness'.

In the fable, the prophet Jonah represents Israel, his name, which means 'dove', now being often given to the Hebrew people. Jonah was in fact a historic figure from an earlier period, briefly mentioned in 2 Kings 14, 25, where it is said that he foretold the conquests of Jereboam II, by which this king restored Israel's territory. Thus his name had an authentically historical ring, yet he was shadowy enough to serve as the central figure in what is almost certainly a purely imaginative fable, and be made to embody the temper of mind which is the author's real subject. Nineveh represents the heathen world, all that part of it which does not recognise holiness or its god. Thus, the work explores the proper attitude of Israel to foreign and unholy peoples generally, rebuking the fanatical extremism of those sacralist prophets, mainly perhaps a group of contemporary zealots, who adopted a boundlessly punitive and destructive one. Over against them, it asserts that the entire world, Israelite and non-Israelite, man and beast, are all alike God's tender concern, fellow participants in the blessing.

Turning to the book itself, it will be remembered how the reluctant Jonah is finally prevailed upon to visit Nineveh, to proclaim God's judgement upon it for its sins, how to the prophet's intense disappointment the Ninevites instantly repent, and how to his anger God then shows clemency to Nineveh. For Jonah, Nineveh is an unholy city which ought therefore to be utterly destroyed, one which is wasting his time if holiness is not thus vindicated. But God now prepares a gourd to shelter Jonah in his grief, then sends a worm to wither the gourd, so that Jonah has no sooner begun to appreciate it than its loss exposes him to sun and wind, so that in retrospect he appreciates it even more. Finally, God gently justifies his mercy, in the moving final words of the poem, which\distil the organic idea that Israelite and non-Israelite, man and beast and plant, are bound together as fellow creatures enjoying the blessing, and bringing blessing to each other, together with the humane spirit which comes from recognising this bond:

> Then saith the Lord, Thou hast had pity on the gourd, for which thou hast not laboured, neither madest it grow; which came up in a night, and perished in a night; And should not I spare Nineveh, that great city, wherein are more than six score thousand persons that cannot discern between their right hand and their left hand; and also much cattle.[47]

God's last, and hopefully most convincing words, turn upon the intolerable thought of destroying not only confused fellow men but also the cattle of Nineveh, those good beasts with whom, under the dispensation of the blessing, man feels himself enrichingly united.

But we are told nothing of the effect of God's words upon Jonah, for the story breaks off abruptly at this point. Nor is it difficult to see why. God's self-justification, expressing the outlook of the poet, may be richly communicative to the reader. Yet it is hard to imagine how it can truly speak to and change the fanatical prophet, or the sacralist Israel he represents, short of some incredible reversal of their ruling assumptions. The organic side of the Hebrew tradition is ever its ethically fertile part, and yet it soon seems destined always to be overwhelmed by an opposed and stronger passion for the Holy, vainly challenging firmly established contrary psychic priorities. The teaching of Jesus stands in the same organic tradition as that of Hosea and the author of Jonah, of which it is indeed the culminating expression, and for many centuries likewise succumbs to sacralism. But of this I shall say more later.

2

THE HEBREW ATTITUDE
TO ANIMALS

We next consider the conflict at the heart of the Hebrew outlook as revealed by certain contradictions in the Hebrew attitude to animals. But first something must be said about what may seem to give undue prominence to a minor matter. Differences in man's reaction to animals are often felt to lie on the very margin of cultural history, a theme best consigned to peripheral monographs. I believe the truth to be quite otherwise. For man's retention or loss of wholeness on his journey into complexity, which in turn so greatly affects the humane quality of his life, is largely determined and vividly shown by his response to the beasts. A *certain* distancing of himself from them, in order to become fully what he is and not only an animal, seems to be the necessary price of advance to civilised achievement. Yet this needful degree of separation is by no means a uniform or inevitable quantity, but rather shows momentous cultural and historic variations, with psychic and ethical repercussions of the first order. In particular, the resultant attitude can be that of a superior and remote overlord, enhancing his sense of unique excellence by setting himself far above and apart from the beasts, and exulting in his mastery over them. Or else, it can be cherishing and companionable, experiencing and teachable, tenaciously keeping vital connection with animals as kindred beings, enriching his life through daily relationship, and guiding him by their simpler but surer integration. Such differences are of the greatest importance for man's conception of himself and crucial for the arrangement of his mental life, being decisive for how much human integrity is disrupted or preserved in the course of the civilising venture; for whether or not the newly strengthened centre keeps in consultative union with the totality it aims to serve. They also provide a window into the soul of a race or age, still more so, I think, than does their choice of heroes. Thus even varying preferences between the beasts, in different cultures and periods, are important as showing the general reaction, if only because some animals lend themselves to a sense of distant superiority in man, while others speak to a longing for intimate nearness. This is why we now turn to the Hebrew response to animals, including their predilections among them. At the same time, its elementary quality may help us to view their formidable legacy respectfully, but without a disabling excess of piety.

1

We find in the literature of the Hebrews, and may safely attribute to their organic side, a persistent strain of immediate feeling and cherishing regard for animals - a response which must owe much to this people's pastoralist origins as nomadic herdsmen, their very movements governed by the needs of their beasts. In the first place, it is repeatedly stressed in the Old Testament that man must tend his animals as fellow living beings, rather than seeing them as endlessly exploitable possessions. The sabbath day of rest is to be enjoyed by ox and ass and all cattle, no less than by servants and strangers within the gate.[1] It is commanded that calf and lamb shall be left for at least seven days with their mothers.[2] Oxen must be allowed to eat the corn which they tread on in threshing: 'Thou shalt not muzzle the ox when he treadeth out the corn.'[3] A man's relationship with his animals is also seen as like that with his own family, for one of the most touching descriptions in the Old Testament is of the poor man and his one dearly loved ewe lamb, to whose seizure by a rich man Nathan compares David's murder of Uriah the Hittite, so that he may take his wife:

> But the poor man had nothing, save one little ewe lamb, which he had brought and nourished up: and it grew up together with him, and with his children; it did eat of his own meat, and drank of his own cup, and lay in his bosom, and was unto him as a daughter.[4]

There could hardly be a more tender evocation of love and intimate companionship between man and beast, even if there is perhaps a touch of hyperbole or sentimentalism in the last phrase. Isaiah of Jerusalem compares the relationship between father and children, as represented by that between Yahweh and his people, with the knowledge which is between man and his animals: 'the ox knoweth his owner, and the ass his master's crib'.[5] At times, the Hebrew is not above learning from animals, even in the area of his closest relationships. He longs for his beloved to emulate the gentler animals, with their tenderness towards their young, their physical demonstrativeness, and their instinct for relating through touch: 'Let her be as the loving hind and pleasant roe.'[6] The Hebrews also show a specially deep feeling for cattle, with their warmth and emotional substantiality - 'the cattle upon a thousand hills'.[7] Much Hebrew writing, then, shows a profound awareness of man's bond with the beasts, and of its precious quality.

The Hebrews likewise pay animals the crucial tribute of seeing them as endowed like men with souls. For the Hebrew mind, the soul is not the immaterial occupant of a body, but all that stamps a living creature with a unique character. When God forms man, and breathes into his nostrils the breath of life, man is not *supplied with* but *becomes* 'a living soul'. It is a profoundly organic conception, not only because it dispenses with the distinction between immaterial and material, the inner and outer essence of a creature, but because it coincides with how our whole being actually registers a man or beast, in natural encounter with them. To us, the once much-debated question whether animals have souls, and if so of what kind, may seem scholastic and unprofitable, because of our doubts about the meaning and usefulness of the term itself. But, without taking sides on that point, there can be no doubt that historically it has often significantly reflected, and influenced, man's esteem or otherwise for the beasts, and whether he has sought to make great or small the distance between himself and them. For instance, Aquinas's certainty that the animal soul is radically inferior in kind to the human, condemning animals to pure desire undisciplined by reason, a life of lust without satisfaction, and will without direction, ministers to his sense of lofty remoteness from them, and his belief that they are made to serve and be ruled by man. To the Hebrews, it seemed evident that animals, no less than men, do have souls, and of the same kind. It followed that they are man's fellow creatures in the full sense, and correspondingly entitled both to respect and solicitude for their needs, an attitude distilled in the great Hebrew saying, 'A righteous man considereth the soul of his cattle.'[8]

In accordance with the same view, when God makes his covenant with Noah and his charges after the Flood, they are all seen as creatures of like nature and substance, with the same claim not to be arbitrarily destroyed:

> And I, behold, I establish my covenant with you, and with your seed after you; and with every living creature that is with you, of the fowl, of the cattle, and of every beast of the earth with you; from all that go out of the ark, to every beast of the earth.[9]

The covenant is made, without distinction of eminence in the scheme of things, with 'every living creature of all flesh that is upon the earth'.[10] The Noah legend's unitive view of man and beast, together with their close relationship there as shipmates, making it a great image distilling one aspect of the blessing, has led later generations, and particularly children, to take it to their hearts, probably more than any other Old Testament story. All this sense of nearness to animals is essentially an expression of wholeness, and a vital means of its renewal. It represents the natural response of the human totality, flowing out to kindred creatures as a rich source of companionship and guidance. And it accounts, I believe, for no small part of the Old Testament's enduring appeal.

2

But the Hebrew attitude to animals has an opposite pole which gradually comes to dominate – a pattern and development to be distinguished from strict linear advance, such as would preclude an early incipient appearance of a characteristically late attitude, or the lingering on of a typically primitive one. It is expressed in tendencies that run completely counter to the organic acknowledgement of man's bond with the beasts. In the first place, there develops a rampant pride of human excellence, in virtue of centralist potency and a unique relationship with the God who confers it, and a consequent belief in man's right and mission to be a lofty tyrant over the animals. In the cosmic creation story attached as a prelude to the largely earlier material of Genesis – and belonging, as was said earlier, to its latest stratum, the Priestly Document – if man is a frail being made of dust, he alone is also granted the supreme honour of being made in God's likeness. And in virtue of standing on that pedestal he is given 'dominion over the fish of the sea, and over the fowl of the air, and over every living thing that moveth upon the earth'.[11] If we are tempted to interpret 'dominion' here as mere humble and caring rule, the exultant ring of the words belies this. And elsewhere it is openly presented as a tyranny of fear. Even in the Noah story, so notable for its stress on unity and comradeliness between man and beast, there is an almost certainly late addition, emphasising man's privilege of intimidating mastery over the beasts. We are told that God promised to Noah, 'And the fear of you and the dread of you shall be upon every beast of the earth.'[12] It is over-whelmingly probable that this incongruous claim to self-elevation through terror represents a gloss by the 'priestly' narrator; for it comes in a 'priestly' section of the story as we have it (which is a skilful blending by a redactor of two earlier renderings of an ancient tale: on the one hand that of the more conservative 'Yahwehist', and on the other that of the late and more doctrinally inclined 'priestly' writer). Whilst we cannot absolutely rule out an early provenance, reflecting the presence already of a strand of contrary feeling towards animals, the priestly writer's theological adjustments of his material are too marked and pervasive for this to be at all likely. It is as if he feels compelled to redress the unity and companionship enjoyed by man and animal in his source, as detracting from proper human superiority and masterfulness.

The felt divine right and duty to tyrannise over the animals is eventually reflected in high-handed schemes for the removal or transformation of certain of them, plans which may suit man but treat the beasts concerned as dispensable, or deny their essential character and needs. For instance, in Ezekiel's vision of future happiness, the beasts of prey are to be exterminated, for Yahweh declares, 'I will make with them a covenant of peace, and will cause the evil beasts to cease out of the land.'[13] In Isaiah of Jesusalem's picture of pacification, on the other hand, the more violent beasts will be conveniently denatured. 'The bear shall graze' and 'the lion shall eat straw like the ox'.[14] Accordantly, when an enemy city is placed under the terrible ban of 'unholy' (*herem*), considered later in another connection, all its animals are to be destroyed, along with its human popul-ation. As regards the beasts, the Hebrews succumb to the barren but heady thrill of dominion. It is a self-promotion and exultation going far beyond recognition of the needful human managerial role in relation to them, the masterly claims and responsibilities of farmer and animal-owner, or acknowledgement of such distancing of them as is necessary for civilisation.

This whole arrogant centralist will to elevate man, and see him as high overlord of animals, is consummated and distilled when the psalmist proclaims:

> What is man, that thou art mindful of him? and the son of man, that thou visitest him? For thou hast made him a little lower than the angels, and has crowned him with glory and honour. Thou madest him to have dominion over the works of thy hands; *thou hast put all things under his feet:* all sheep and oxen, yea, and the beasts of the field; the fowl of the air, and the fish of the sea, and whatsoever passeth through the paths of the seas.[15]

We are reminded of the rationalistic Sophocles' paean in praise of man, the wonder of the world, lord of the earth and subjugator of the beasts, through his cleverness and craft:

> Many wonders there are, and yet none is more wonderful than man . . . With woven nets he snares the race of thoughtless birds, the tribes of savage beasts, the sea-brood of the deep, this man of subtle wit. By his cunning he masters the animals that nest in the wilderness, that roam across the hills; he tames the rich-maned horse, putting a yoke upon its neck, and the unwearied mountain bull.[16]

Indeed, even the extreme anthropocentric arrogance of the ultra-rationalistic Renaissance, which sees man as like an angel in apprehension, the beauty of the world and paragon of animals, and the ruler of nature, hardly goes further. In sum, the Hebrews come mainly to regard man, not as a fellow creature living in the midst of animals, albeit with a need and duty to care for and control, but as a super-creature exalted over them. This attitude also, in conjunction

with the factors mentioned earlier, helped the eventual fusion
of Judaism and Hellenism.

3

Along with this mounting sense of human supremacy, and
pride of mastery over the beasts, there also grows the
tendency which later so sorely impoverished and denatured
the medieval response to animals: the will to treat them as
sacramental or symbolic, agents of a theological scheme,
leading men to look not at but through them to a grander
horizon. Superficially, it may seem an enhancement of
status, but this is by no means so. In the last analysis, we
rightly tend to have little time for the derivatively valuable
and second-rate, the mere outskirts of the immeasurably
better, while we are distanced from what we subordinate to
a greater concern. As Israel's god comes to be credited with
the creation of the world, animals begin to be seen primarily
as high works of the Lord, miracles of divine power and
craftmanship, proclaiming the might and skill of the creator.
They become first and foremost aspects of the stupendous
coup de théâtre of creation. At the same time, they merge
into a view of the world as a vast aesthetic treasure-house and
visual spectacle, a perpetual reminder of the wonderful
creative act, one which ever compels awe of the god who
performed it. The essential attitude is beautifully captured in
the words which the three Archangels address to the Lord,
near the beginning of Goethe's *Faust*,

> Der Anblick gibt den Engeln Stärke,
> Da keiner dich ergründen mag,
> Und alle deine hohen Werke
> Sind herrlich wie am ersten Tag.

[The spectacle (of Creation) gives strength to angels,
since none can fathom you, and all your high creations
are glorious as on the first day.]

This whole vision is distilled when the psalmist cries:

> O Lord, how manifold are thy works! in wisdom hast
> thou made them all: the earth is full of thy riches . . .
> The glory of the Lord shall endure for ever: the Lord
> shall rejoice in his works.[17]

Its detailed unfolding comes in the Book of Job, where Job
is overwhelmed by the cumulative magnificence of the divine
handiwork, the wild ass 'whose house I have made the
wilderness',[18] the horse 'who paweth in the valley, and
rejoiceth in his strength',[19] and much else in the natural
world besides. All these wonderfully beautiful creations
point, away from themselves, to the splendour of their
creator. Von Rad observes: 'But we must say this: admittedly the objects thus contemplated are all perfectly real
things belonging to our world, but this *delectari* of Israel
was not for their own sake, but only as they became visible
in their reality in the context of faith, in their relationship to
God.'[20]

Thus, the beasts come to serve the clothing of their maker
with honour and majesty. It is a process of thought essential
to the magnifying of a creator-god, but it is also one which
works against an intimate, an experiencing and consultative
relationship with them. As a lightly superimposed idea and
belief, perhaps it can sometimes bring an added thankfulness
and regard. But as a dominant conception, controlling man's
whole view of animals, it is at odds with an immediate and
cherishing response to them, in and for themselves.

4

An unfortunate but telling side-effect of this increasingly
theological, and instrumental, concern with the beasts was a
growing preoccupation with those whose ferocity and
strength most manifests the fearful power of nature, and so

both of her supposed creator and his Hebrew beneficiaries – animals with whom, for this very reason, man wisely seldom forms close relationships, and that with limited success. Accordingly, we find praise of Behemoth, whose 'bones are as strong pieces of brass', and of Leviathan, whom no man can bind for his little girls.[21] Above all, there develops a fixation upon the eagle and the lion. Calling to Moses out of the mountain, Yahweh commands him to tell the children of Israel 'how I bare you on eagle's wings, and brought you unto myself'.[22] In the Song of Moses, a theodicy vindicating the ways of Israel's god, the poet exultantly recalls that Yahweh once led his people 'As an eagle stirreth up her nest, fluttereth over her young, spreadeth abroad her wings, taketh them, beareth them on her wings'.[23] In virtue of this eagle-like nature and relationship with his people, the writer goes on to tell us, the Lord made Israel 'ride on the high places of the earth'. 'Thus saith Yahweh', Jeremiah proclaims, foretelling the utter destruction of the Moabites, 'Behold, he shall fly as an eagle, and shall spread his wings over Moab.'[24] When the comforter Elihu seeks to bludgeon Job into humility before divine providence, by rehearsing the wonders of God's creative power, his climactic example is the eagle:

> Doth the eagle mount up at thy command, and make her nest on high? She dwelleth and abideth on the rock, upon the crag of the rock, and the strong place. From thence she seeketh the prey, and her eyes behold afar off.[25]

In the Book of Proverbs, 'the way of an eagle in the air' is felt to be one of the four most wonderful things.[26] Aspiring to be like their god, the Hebrews see their ideal selves in the same image of the eagle, trusting that they that wait upon the Lord 'shall mount up with wings as eagles'.[27] Truly, the eagle was a perfect symbol of the lofty and majestic god of Israel. As well as its proud strength, its amazing swiftness of stoop, and its lordship over other birds, there is its partiality for giddy heights and its habit of circling radiant summits. It is also perennially dear to those who would make themselves mighty through sheer force of will, as we are reminded by the Habsburgs' predilection for it.

But the lion enjoys even greater prominence in Hebrew writing, as an expression of divine glory and Israelite strength, making over a hundred appearances in the Old Testament. 'The Lion hath roared, who will not fear? the Lord God hath spoken, who can but prophesy?' Amos proclaims.[28] Likewise, Hosea represents God as promising, 'I will be unto Ephraim as a lion, and as a young lion to the house of Judah',[29] or again, 'I will be unto them as the lion',[30] while the prophet declares that when the Lord's people walk after him, 'He shall roar like a lion: when he shall roar, then the children shall tremble from the West.'[31] In the Book of Proverbs, foremost among the four things which are 'comely in going' is 'the lion which is strongest among beasts, and turneth not away for any'.[32] As with the eagle, the Hebrews like to think of themselves as the same lion by which they image forth their god. Israel lies down 'as a lion, and as a great lion';[33] and is a lion's whelp.[34] As we have seen, far from caring for lions in and for themselves, the Hebrews apparently longed either to get rid of the beasts of prey, or else to change their nature beyond recognition. But the lion's supreme combination of strength and majesty was indisputable, and so it had to be extolled as emblem of a mighty and majestic god, and of his irresistibly potent chosen people. Inevitably, the image of eagle and lion are sometimes combined. Of those ideal heroes Saul and Jonathan, we are told that 'they were swifter than eagles, they were stronger than lions',[35] while Ezekiel has a vision of the divine chariot, in which its every wheel has four faces: those of a cherub, a man, a lion and an eagle.[36] If all this theologically directed and self-extolling admiration of animals, with its concentration upon those best suited to the purpose, shows a delight in them as fearfully and wonderfully made, it also essentially diminishes the beasts. For it subordinates them to a grander concern, and so gratuitously distances them, while it gives central importance to ones with whom true relationship is virtually impossible.

5

Finally, the centralist Hebrew remoteness from animals, and its growing dominance, are reflected in their haughtily administrative dietetic distinctions and prohibitions. A formative factor here is a dread of adulterating the racial psyche, by assimilating into the personality, through eating them, the psychic quality of incompatible or disapproved of beasts. 'Ye shall not make your souls abominable by beast . . . which I have separated from you as unclean.'[37] Dietetic abhorrence expresses and enforces psychological fear and withdrawal, and accordingly animals whose meat is unclean are themselves to be regarded as 'an abomination unto you'.[38] But the more fundamental cause is the sacralism which required this obsessive preservation, in undiluted purity, of a special and isolated Hebrew identity. For the dietetic laws of Leviticus are expressly coupled with the injunction 'Ye shall therefore sanctify yourselves, and ye shall be holy, for I am holy', or again, 'And ye shall be holy unto me, for I Yahweh am holy'.[39] We have seen that the concept of holiness turns upon an exaltation of the exceptional and segregated, and that accordingly it defines itself as the negation of the common and dispersed. Thus its underlying principle was satisfied by having a small and special group of acceptable meats and animals, and by excluding from it those associated with other peoples.

Animals come to be rigidly divided into clean and unclean. Ox and sheep and goat are clean, because through long familiarity and service they have long been psychologically absorbed, and so transformed, as it were, into semi-Israelites. The horse and ass are not clean, apparently because the ass was only appropriated shortly after the immigration into Canaan, while the horse was introduced from abroad by Solomon, with the result that they are both, so to speak, only half-absorbed probationary Israelites. The pig is peculiarly unclean, mainly as being the favourite sacrificial animal of the unholy and idolatrous Canaanites,[40] although its notorious indifference to purity must surely have been an influence also. Thus, the Hebrews estranged themselves from a good beast, with whom most entire adults and normal children feel a special if often unavowed affinity, and which Corot did not hesitate to make the central figure in his great realisation of human integrity, *Saint-André-en-Morvan* (where the human couple, who are walking down the lane which leads up to the village, pause to look at a pig, which is exploring the base of the tree at the centre of the landscape).[41] In the biblical version of the story of Noah, the priestly writer feels compelled to add, in an obvious gloss to his original tale, that seven pairs of each species of 'clean' beasts were saved aboard the ark, but only one pair of 'unclean' ones.[42]

By the same token, psychologically dangerous parts of animals are forbidden food. Pre-eminently, blood must not be eaten, for the blood of an animal is its soul – 'the soul of all flesh is its blood'[43] – so that to partake of it carries the risk of a degrading intake of animal nature, a retrogression into animality. A related phenomenon was the growing unrealistic fear of species pollution, culminating in the Deuteronomic prohibition against different animals even being yoked to the same plough.[44] There is here a deep distrust of animal nature, as liable to betray a perfect scheme if left to its own devices. The subtler ramifications of Hebrew dietetic law need not concern us here. All this arrogant legislation regarding animals (and their parts), separating them into psychologically innocuous and harmful, and prescribing their reproductive pattern, in accordance with preconceived ideals, could only enhance the Hebrew sense of man's distance from the beasts, and of his right to make them serve him and his designs.[45]

At the heart of the Hebrew attitude to animals, then, we find contrariety and division: on the one hand, a tender esteem and sense of kinship; on the other and ever more dominant, a most alienating hauteur which throws away the rich rewards of keeping close to them. The Hebrews were torn between a humbly cherishing and a loftily superior response to animals. But when it came to the issue, they were ready mostly to give up nearness to the beasts, and all the fullness of being that flows from it, for territorial acquisition and aggrandisement. For these overriding compulsions demanded a potentiating centralism, which in turn required them to see themselves as the remote overlords of lowlier creatures, and to make these agents of a high scheme originating in the mind of man.

3

THE POETIC FORMS OF
THE HEBREWS

Finally, we examine the dichotomy at the centre of the Hebrew outlook as reflected in the main poetic images of the Hebrews. The overriding pure centralism in the Hebrews, like that of the Greeks, supported and enforced itself through congenial and beautiful poetic forms, which made it imaginatively appealing and psychically insidious, able to speak to man's creative side and infiltrate every level of the mind. These images not only greatly strengthened the hold of the Hebrews' predominant psychology upon themselves. They also did much to win over the Western mind to Hebrew centralism, and to ensure its long ascendancy there, while their elusive influence makes the causes of that dominance hard to unravel. I believe that the key role of such imaginative structures, in the war of ideas as a whole, has been sorely underestimated. For they have a fullness of persuasive power denied to mere assertion and argument, which seldom really touch or possess the soul. To return to the Hebrews, it would be wrong, it seems to me, to think here in terms of a conscious conspiracy to manipulate other societies and generations. Rather, just as individuals naturally seek to realise and develop, strengthen and justify, their own outlook by expressing it imaginatively, so it is natural for peoples to treat thus their central axioms, through specially powerful imaginative expression. And the heightened urge to self-expression shades imperceptibly into the craving to impress and missionary ambition. Moreover, there was in both the Hebrews and Greeks a strain of psychic imperialism, stemming partly from pride of elevation in virtue of their centralist psychologies, a certainty of being set above and apart by this sovereign achievement, and partly from the over-encouraged centre's own appetite for aggrandisement, a strain which made them want all the world to see the unique glory of their point of view, and feel it baulked of its full splendour while any did not do so. This combination of pressures inevitably tends to call forth imperious and communicative poetic forms. The dominant great images of the Hebrews are centralist to the core, but we shall see that the organically leaning Hebrew underside also was not to be denied poetic expression.

1

The poetry of the Hebrews, again like that of the Greeks, is dominated by mountains. In the first place, there towers over Hebrew thought the supremely holy mountain, Sinai or Horeb, scene of God's cardinal revelation of himself to Moses, of his main covenant with his people, and of his handing down to them of their central laws. As well as being invested with uniquely awesome associations, Sinai is felt to be a mountain that shrinks and trembles, shaken to its inmost being by becoming the place on earth where Yahweh has most fully dwelt awhile:

Even Sinai itself was moved at the presence of God, the God of Israel.[1]

In the monarchial period, not a little of this ambience is assumed by holy Mount Zion, 'the mountain of the Lord' and 'the beauteous holy mountain', site of the royal temple:

Yet have I set my King upon my holy hill of Zion.[2]

But there are in the Old Testament some two hundred references to mountains, mostly with ecstatic or numinous overtones. Hebrew poetry is saturated with images, impassioned and unforgettable, which point the mind to radiant summits:

> How beautiful upon the mountains are the feet of him that bringeth good tidings . . .[3]

> Who shall ascend into the hill of the Lord? or who shall stand in his holy place?[4]

> I will lift up mine eyes unto the hills, from whence cometh my help.[5]

> His foundation is in the holy mountains.[6]

> Let them shout from the top of the mountains, give glory to the Lord.[7]

> The beauty of Israel is slain upon thy high places . . .[8]

All these are effectively sister peaks to Olympus and Helicon, having a broadly similar imaginative force. If we are tempted to mis-ascribe this tremendous emphasis on mountains simply to their physical presence, and familiarity as an element in Hebrew and Greek experience, we need only recall that mountains feature but rarely in Latin poetry, despite the centrality of the Apennines and nearness of the Alps.

The essential function of all this mountain imagery – a direction of the mind, mainly at a subconscious level, towards what is uncompromisingly high, and far above and apart from nature, in other words the holy god, and thus towards the high minded centralism which he enforces – is most openly and tellingly revealed in Ezekiel's vision of 'a high mountain and eminent', on the top of which there grows an extraordinary divine tree. This tree is exalted by

Yahweh above all common trees. It eclipses them, and is rendered utterly distinct in nature, by being made of a dry topmost bough, thus forgoing reliance upon natural forms and organic processes, and even the life-giving sap which makes other trees green and tall. In consequence, Yahweh is able to proclaim its total supremacy:

And all the trees of the field shall know that I the Lord have brought down the high tree, have exalted the low tree, have dried up the green tree, and have made the dry tree to flourish: I the Lord have spoken and done it.[9]

Ezekiel's divine tree, towering above all ordinary trees from a summit, and keeping them the more in place by independence of their vital structure, is a classic case of distortion of a natural form for religious ends. Its extreme separation, both physical and biological, make it a holy tree *par excellence*. Plainly, the top of a mountain is the precisely appropriate site for it. For the unnatural tree and the mountain here harmonise and reinforce each other, uniting perfectly to set forth the essential principles of holiness: sovereign isolation and disconnection from the natural world. At the same time, the exact congruity of Ezekiel's anti-natural tree brings home what in the mountain image generally, together with commanding height, makes it an ideal centralist one, namely dissociation from all living nature below. If Ezekiel's vision is unsympathetic, it also has a fierce honesty and consistency which compel respect. For he faces in all its absoluteness the incompatibility of sacralism with its radical opposite, the organic attitude consummated in the idea of the blessing.

The mountain imagery of the Hebrews, as well as being a strong centralist influence upon themselves, also proved so for European culture generally. For it joined with the essentially similar mountain imagery of the Greeks, which was also an agent of their rationalistic form of centralism.

Accordingly, when Milton fuses Hebrew Sinai and Zion with Greek Helicon in his lines

> Sing Heav'nly Muse, that on the secret top
> Of *Oreb*, or of *Sinai*, didst inspire
> That Shepherd, who first taught the chosen Seed,
> In the Beginning how the Heav'ns and Earth
> Rose out of *Chaos:* Or if *Sion* Hill
> Delight thee more, and *Siloa's* Brook that flowd
> Fast by the Oracle of God; I thence
> Invoke thy aid to my adventrous Song,
> That with no middle flight intends to soar
> Above th'*Aonian* Mount . . .[10]

he only makes explicit a union inevitably consummated long before, through centuries of mutually supportive and cognate effects upon the European mind. For these majestic images, setting forth the sovereign power of that which is high, and separate from the natural and animal level, to confer human fulfilment, have a bemusing and intoxicating quality. Thus, they are able to win and enthral the whole personality to pure centralism, a consuming wish for despotic government by the higher faculties, accompanied by a sense that its rightness is somehow echoed and proclaimed by the awesomeness of nature's majestically uplifted places, set apart from her other productions, and appropriately visited but rarely and by few. We may feel that the imaginatively entrancing should always serve the true and helpful, but it does not.

Because of their austere monotheism, it was not open to the Hebrews, as it was to the Greeks, decisively to harness the exploratory and creative life of man to this mountain syndrome, and thus to the centralism which it expressed and enforced, by ascribing inspiration to poetic mountain-dwelling Muses. And so they relied here instead on equivalent and comparably effective – if less beautiful – images, which later joined with the Muses to enforce the same essential view: the prophet as receiver of messages from on high, and the angels who visit man to inspire him from above.

2

The prophet seemingly represents a coalescence of the more or less calmly articulate nomadic seer, the patriachal visionary, with the sanctuary-based ecstatic whom the Israelites encountered in Palestine, combining the potency of both.[11] There is a close connection between early prophecy and magic. The early prophet is largely a sacral instrument of war, a focus of holy potency, a kind of secret weapon. By his presence and support he gives his people psychic strength in conflict, while his semi-magical maledictions weaken that of the enemy. Futuristic insight merges with the conferring of military prowess or weakness, foretelling victory or defeat with ensuring them. Similarly, the prophet is credited with miraculously curing sickness, and restoring to life, causing bears to attack people or lightning to strike them. Increasingly, however, the prophet emerges as before all else a divine man (often literally *elohim*-man) set apart from others, who is granted, in virtue of that promotion and separation, momentous messages from on high. What a prophet's own heart tells him is always carefully distinguished from his characteristic great pronouncements, which are divinely given. He typically undergoes the rare and secret experience of a call, or admission into the presence of God, delivering him from human inadequacies. In doing so, he is seen as following in lowlier fashion his supreme exemplar, Moses, who actually met God on a mountain-top. Commonly, his moments of creative insight come to him in the form of a vision (in other words the antithesis of a poetic process rooted in, and arising from, the everyday life of our whole being and the common experience of all, such as produces a proverb or parable or richly expressive concrete and homely image), and only to a rare few blessed with this capability. The essential idea is captured when the prophet declares, 'I stand upon my watch and set me upon a fortress to see what he will say in me.'[12]

It is increasingly expected that the prophet will always express himself in incantatory language, a tone and style that eventually leads or allows his words to be seen as holy writ. Lastly, he often emphasises his isolated access to the divine by peculiar and uncanny symbolic actions, earlier the ritual dance, and later such motions as unaccountably trembling and lying motionless.[13] All this makes the prophet a looming and awful figure, who tends to haunt and intimidate the ordinary mind. Assuredly, he does not encourage doubt that inspiration is best thought of as supramundane in origin, a gift from heaven to the correspondingly lofty in man, whether that is the case or no. Not only did the Hebrew conception of the prophet powerfully express and enforce the heavenward-looking centralism of the Hebrews. His select status and inspirational pattern, having much in common with those of oracles and sibyls and poets visited by Muses, also did much to ease the convergence of Judaism and Hellenism. Thus, when Michelangelo designed the Sistine ceiling, conceived as a hymn and a majestically impressive monument to the spirit that confers creative wisdom from above, he made brooding Hebrew prophets alternate with the Delphic and other sibyls, as being twin expressions of essentially the same view of inspiration.

In Hebrew literature, creative insight is also given to man by angels, superior beings whose rare and sudden materialisation, or invisible presence, giving knowledge beyond the mind's normal scope, epitomises the principle of inspiration from remotest heaven. In early times, this insistence that inspiration comes from above was less pronounced than later, yet already strongly prefigured. For it will be remembered that Jacob's most creatively inspired moment comes to him, not on a mountain-top or from a heavenly messenger, but in a dream while his head is laid on a low-lying pile of stones, albeit not a little promoted by being quite exceptional ones – so much so indeed that Jacob afterwards sets them up as a pillar, pours oil upon it, and names it 'God's house'.[14] Even so, the terrestrial bias of the story already has to be redressed by the dominant features of Jacob's dream: a ladder whose top reaches to heaven, and upon it, ascending and descending, angel messengers. The power and vertical thrust of the image are familiar to us from the art of William Blake. The notion of the angel evolves toward ever closer association with inspiration from on high.

To begin with, an angel tends to take the visible form of a man, probably representing a theophany or direct manifestation of God, as when three such heavenly visitants in human shape tell Abraham that his aged wife Sarah will bear a child, or when another informs Manoah's wife that she will bear a son, the mighty Nazarite Samson:

> Then the woman came and told her husband, saying, 'A man of God came to me, and his countenance was like the countenance of an angel of God, very terrible: but I asked him not whence he was, neither told he me his name: But he said .unto me, Behold thou shalt conceive and bear a son.'[15]

Later, as Israel's god grows more remote, the angel becomes a doubtfully visible and certainly superhuman figure, a high servant dwelling before the face of Yahweh and forming part of his court, who may be sent on an earthly mission to inspire and guide, even bearing within him the sacred name of the Lord:

> Behold, I send an Angel before thee, to keep thee in the way, and to bring thee into the place which I have prepared. Beware of him, and obey his voice, provoke him not; for he will not pardon your transgressions: for my name is in him.[16]

From the time of Ezekiel onwards, the ever greater stress on divine transcendence enhances the importance of angels as mediators, and they are assigned specific functions, such as protection and punishment. They enter still more into their own as bearers of inspiration in the Book of Daniel, written during the years 167–164 BC, in the considerably Hellenised Jerusalem of the Antiochan oppression, to encourage the Jews to be loyal to their faith in face of this persecution. Daniel has the dream vision of the four beasts explained to him by an angel, is given the meaning of his dream of the ram and he-goat by Gabriel, is visited by him again to clarify Jeremiah's prophecy of punishment to Babylon in 'seventy years', and has a final vision communicated by an angel when he is awake.[17] Finally, angels gain fully developed status in the elaborate angelical system of the Essene movement that emerged about 150 BC, and which influenced both the Greek-speaking Judaism of the Dispersion and early Christianity. Here the hierarchy of angels at once serves a rationalised picture of God, and compensates for the final distancing of him which it entails, becoming forerunners of the Plotinian system of intermediate beings who span the gulf between the Good and the particular world. The persistence of the link between angels and inspiration is illustrated by the fact that Savonarola consistently claimed that his visions were formed 'by God through the ministration of angels . . . spirits who not only inform and arouse the imagination internally towards various apparitions, but also address the prophets from within'.[18] To the imaginative force of these always poetic beings a great body of European art bears witness. As well as being key elements in a theological system, the concepts of prophet and angel were both great poetic forms, upholding and enforcing the sacralist vision.

3

Yet for all their obsession with mountains, and related human and superhuman figures, the stubbornly enduring organic underside of the Hebrews would not allow them to forget a very different region, namely the water's edge. The psychic need in man to frequent the water-side is profoundly organic: it is something that arises from our whole being – not, like the urge to ascend mountains, from our higher faculties alone – for it is a natural place for us, rather than one of pilgrimage for our loftier selves; our impulse to linger there is also one which we share with the beasts, most of whom do not care much for mountains. We may recall here not only animals watering but how dogs love to play at the sea's edge, or by the sides of rivers. In literature and art, we may think of Theocritus' sharply observed description of a dog by the sea, 'Ah see how he barks as he runs along the shore through the gentle foam',[19] or the precisely appropriate dogs by the shore in Piero di Cosimo's *Mythological Scene*, or the ecstatic dog at the edge of the river in Constable's sketch for *The Haywain*.* I believe that this acutely poetic terrain – the margin between the familiar habitat of land and the strange, the formless and illimitable element of water – has far-reaching implications which cannot be pursued here. Elsewhere, I argue that it is the true and natural metaphor both of the origin of inspiration and man's creative life and of the mental region where his explorative side properly finds fulfilment; and that this is first adequately set forth in Shakespeare's *The Tempest*, that great exploration of imaginative power and its sources, where the water-side and its divinities take on once more their rightful importance.† But that is another story. It will suffice here to notice the

* While retaining much of the dog's happiness in the *Haywain* itself, Constable makes it more dignified, and more interested in the human figures at the centre of the landscape.

† In *The Paradise Myth* (1969), and in my forthcoming study *Poetic Rationalism and the Renaissance*.

radically organic provenance of the need to frequent the water's edge, and of the profound appeal of images which present this region.

The Hebrews did not forget this marginal area, or neglect sometimes to respond to its attraction. For instance, they situated the oracle of God near Siloa's brook, and poured libations from its spring. But, more important, some of the most haunting lines in Hebrew poetry are concerned with that territory:

> As the hart panteth after the waterbrooks, so panteth my soul after thee, O God.[20]

Or,

> There is a river, the streams whereof shall make glad the city of God . . .[21]

Or again,

> He leadeth me beside the still waters.[22]

Or once more,

> By the rivers of Babylon, there we sat down, yea, we wept, when we remembered Zion.[23]

Such words still have power to touch those who do not believe in Hebrew religion, and have little love for Sinai or Olympus.

The opposition in Hebrew poetry between centralist mountain imagery and organic images of the water-side bears further witness to the persistent conflict at the heart of the Hebrew outlook. It also shows again how the preferred centralist intent overwhelmingly prevails. For images of the water-side are a recessive element in Hebrew literature. Not only are they quantitatively eclipsed by the omnipresent mountain imagery, they also typically express an exceptional moment of contemplative insight, or an elegiac feeling of loss and separation, as if the Hebrew mind tended to turn to this region mainly in instants of rare intuition, or in downcast and negative ones, when it felt obscurely that its high-minded centralism had somehow let it down, and the god of that psychic system seemed intolerably far away. Consequently, the Hebrew images of the water-side lack the confidence and strength which speak to the ambitious, qualities which the towering mountain imagery possesses in abundance. Thus, their influence on the Hebrew mind was correspondingly small. And when it came to shaping the European tradition here too they cut little ice.

4

HEBREW SACRALISM AND THE HUMANE RESPONSE

1

Finally, we consider the ethical consequences of the Hebrews' overriding sacralist centralism, with its supportive, ever more uplifted and isolated god. But, before we turn to these in detail, something must be said about two closely related matters: the general quality of the Hebrew humane response and the lofty moral idealism that is so marked a feature of later Hebrew thought. To begin with the first, under the dispensation of Mosaic Yahwism, the Hebrews seem at no stage to have been a particularly humane people, nor yet equipped easily to become one, by which I do not of course imply that they are singular in this respect. Even where they are most generous, namely in their earlier tolerance towards the stranger in their midst (of which I shall say more presently), 'because we too were bondsmen in Egypt', the nationalistic aspect of the reaction tends to overshadow the kindly. The stranger is principally tolerated as a semi-Israelite, a peripheral part of the national psyche, through sharing the historic experience of Israel, rather than simply as a fellow human being. More generally, Hebrew humanitarianism is restricted primarily by a ruthless centralism that disrupts integrity, the fount of a truly humane response, but hardly less by a dominance of theological objectives, and a subordination of the poor and oppressed to these. Essentially, it is the same preference of the theological level to the factual in the ethical sphere, the moral emigration from earthly concerns to heavenly ones, that we shall meet later in the patristic age and the Middle Ages, when they once more thin and stunt humanitarian feeling and activity.

True, it is repeatedly stressed that Yahweh has a partiality for the weak and miserable, which he expresses by intervening to transform their lot. But it is also made equally plain that this bias in favour of the dependent lowly, those who wait for his mercy, is essentially the reverse of his antipathy towards the independently strong and happy, who threaten his monopoly of these blessings. Thus, to raise up the lowly is the most conclusive way to bring down the objectionable mighty, while at the same time showing his total supremacy over nature. Basically, it is the same logic of aggrandisement that leads Yahweh to make the dry branch tower unnaturally over all naturally green and tall trees, as we saw earlier, or again to exalt every valley and make low the mountains and hills. Certainly, the main motive is not distress at weakness and misery in themselves, since these are cause for positive jubilation when redistributed so as to glorify the one holy god. Repeatedly, we meet the same doubtful pattern of benevolence: promoting the weak, to demote the strong, to elevate the Holy One. 'For thou wilt save the afflicted people, but wilt bring down high looks.'[1] 'He poureth contempt upon princes, and causeth them to wander in the wilderness, where there is no way, yet setteth he the poor on high from affliction, and maketh him families like a flock.'[2] This barren ethic of divine promotion through reversing human fortunes is distilled, and expressed most fully and candidly, in Hannah's hymn of praise:

> The bows of the mighty men are broken, and they that stumbled are girded with strength. They that were full have hired out themselves for bread; and they that were hungry ceased; so that the barren hath born seven; and she that hath many children is waxed feeble . . . Yahweh maketh poor and maketh rich: he bringeth low, and lifteth up. He raiseth up the poor out of the

dust, and lifteth up the beggar from the dunghill, to set them among princes, and to make them inherit the throne of glory.[3]

The stumbling and hungry, the barren and poor, are here raised up not from tender concern for their plight but to show the power of Yahweh to humiliate other possible contenders for success and greatness: the strong and full, the fertile and wealthy.

Assuredly, this way of thinking promotes awe of the Holy One. It may also have incidentally improved somewhat the status and prospects of the unfortunate, yet they stood to gain little from it, not being its real concern. But essentially it is alien and contrary to the humanitarian impulse and spirit of reform. The poor and wretched are treated as instruments of sacralism and agents of a religious and psychic scheme. Admittedly, as well as the exceptionally tender description of the poor Uriah and his one ewe-lamb, there are also a number of thin general injunctions not to oppress, and even to aid, the helpless – such as the Deuteronomic command not to exploit the fatherless and widow,[4] Isaiah's more positive 'Judge the fatherless, plead for the widow',[5] the proverb 'Happy is he who hath mercy on the poor',[6] and the psalmist's 'blessed is he that considereth the poor'.[7] But these sentiments are far from frequent, carry relatively little weight of emotion – much less than the soon to be considered denunciations of those who oppress the poor – and, most important, lack the crucial feeling for specific miseries. We miss in them the main roots and marks of true humanitarian feeling: the flow of kindly sympathy towards a particular distressed fellow creature, the sense of shared distinct vulnerabilities, and most of all the pained awareness of *concrete sufferings and deprivations*, the torn garment which will not be mended, the shiver of cold that might be our own.

At this point, I think it will be helpful if we briefly contrast the Hebrew humane response with that of the much earlier Sumerians, that deeply civilised people whose organic approach to the sophistication of religion we have already considered, and, incidentally, the only other one in the ancient Near East to have left a sizeable literary record on which to base such a contrast. Before turning to the Sumerian proverbs which are the real point of the comparison, we should note that certain Sumerian rulers have left a notable record of caring and systematic social reform. We know this, in the first place, from the tablets recording the reforms of Urukagina, ruler of Lagash in the twenty-fourth century BC, following a period when the poor had suffered much injustice and exploitation at the hands of the rich, but probably reviving laws of an earlier age which had fallen into disuse. The laws of Urukagina were directed not only to curbing bureaucratic excesses but also to protecting the humble from oppression by the wealthy and powerful. They prescribed that 'if a poor man's son laid out a fishing pond, no one would now steal its fish', that no wealthy official might trespass in the garden of a 'poor man's mother' to carry off its fruit, and that no superior might buy a poor man's house or ass at an unfair price or against his will. Urukagina also made a special covenant with Ningirsu, the patron-god of Lagash, that he would not allow the widow and orphan to be victimised by the 'men of power'.[8] Similar objectives were embraced by the law code of Ur-Nammu, founder of the Third Dynasty of Ur, in about 2050 BC, which provided that 'the orphan was not given over to the powerful, the man of 1 shekel was not given over to the man of mina'.[9] None of these reforms may have endured long, and we know that the reign of Urukagina lasted only ten years, before Lagash was overwhelmed by the aggressive neighbouring state of Umora. Nevertheless, they bear witness to a widespread will to practical humanity, for such measures by a ruler are nearly always a joint product of his own determination and the wishes of many of the ruled. The fact of their enactment and the presence of a psychology and moral climate that favoured them are finally more important,

I think, than their unknown scale and efficacy.

Such humanitarianism comes as no surprise in view of the humane amplitude that pervades Sumerian literature. There is, for instance, the moving deep grief of Gilgamesh at the loss of his half-animal friend and *alter ego* Enkidu, which drives him to embark, not like the similarly bereaved Achilles on an orgy of vacuous revenge, but on a searchingly reflective if vain quest for the secret of eternal life:

> O Enkidu, my brother . . .
> What is this sleep which holds you now?
> You are lost in the dark and cannot hear me[10]

Again, there is the climactic message of *The Epic of Gilgamesh*, that man cannot escape death, but that life's profoundest fulfilments are too rich and good to spoil or miss by constantly brooding on the sad fact of mortality:

> Gilgamesh, where are you hurrying to? You will never find that everlasting life for which you are looking. When the gods created man they allotted to him death, but life they retained in their own keeping . . . Let your clothes be fresh, bathe yourself in water, cherish the little child that holds your hand, and make your wife happy in your embrace; for this too is the lot of man.[11]

Or, once more, there is the grave simplicity of Inanna-Ishtar's words in the poem telling of her sacred wedding to Dumuzzi-Tammuz:

> Let them join his hand in my hand,
> Let them join his heart to my heart,
> Sweet is it to sleep hand in hand with him,
> And equally good the loveliness of joining heart to heart.[12]

The poetry of the Sumerians communicates a rich and tender humanity, with which their humanitarian record is in keeping.

But far more significant are certain Sumerian proverbs,

which show a distressed and immediate awareness of the degrading hardships and humiliations of poverty, in their pressing actuality, a theme to which they insistently return:

> How the poor man is diminished!
> The edge of the oven is his mill;
> His ripped garment will not be mended;
> What he has lost will not be sought for.

Or,

> By his debts the poor man is brought low;
> What is snatched from his mouth must repay his debts.

Or,

> A poor man strains his eyes towards what he will have to eat.

Or again,

> A poor man worries about what he has borrowed.

Or once more,

> The poor are the silent ones of the land.[13]

This is the warm and ethically kindling language of pain at the concrete miseries of destitution, not the cold and morally anaesthetising one of general pronouncements arising from abstract schemes. Not until the great humanitarian and reformist upsurge of the eighteenth century – among whose leading spokesmen are Fielding and Johnson and Blake, and later Hood and Dickens – and this is surely an extraordinary fact, do we find it widely spoken again; although in due course we shall notice its crucial contribution in an incipient form, or rather that of the response that gives rise to it, to tentative humanitarian growth in the later Middle Ages. It likewise underlies Shakespeare's deep compassion in *King Lear*, so exceptional for its time:

> How shall your houseless heads and unfed sides,
> Your loopt and window'd raggedness, defend you
> From seasons such as these?

For it makes all the difference in the world whether our fellows' sufferings are sharply felt in all their particularity, with immediate pity, or distanced and diminished by subordination to high general conceptions. In the idiom of Augustan benevolism, Fielding well sums up the basic principle when he writes:

> Good nature is that benevolent and amiable temper of mind which disposes us to *feel the misfortunes and enjoy the happiness* of others, and consequently pushes us on to promote the latter and prevent the former; and that without any abstract contemplation on the beauty of virtue, and without the allurements and terrors of religion.[14]

He also applied it in his words and tracts, and particularly in his *Proposal for Making an Effective Provision for the Poor* (1753).

Now I have no wish to idealise the Sumerians. Nevertheless, this embryo of authentic humanitarianism is persistently present in the Sumerian proverbs, a natural fruit of the organic outlook of the Sumerians, who, we have seen, sought to preserve integrity by keeping their newly elevated and humanised deities still near to nature, as well as by maintaining vital connection with the beasts. But it is conspicuously lacking in the Old Testament. As well as throwing this humane deficiency into relief, the Sumerian comparison – coming from a period at least a thousand years earlier than Genesis – may also save us from the progressivism that mistakenly sees Old Testament inhumanity as somehow inevitable, so early in history.

2

When we seek to assess the ethical consequences of Hebrew sacralism, we must carefully distinguish the actual humane developments from the career of moral idealism, and of the denunciation of wickedness; for these last are not a reliable index of the humane pattern and its progress. We remember how Hesiod magnified divine justice and fervently denounced exploitation and disunity in the strife-ridden Greece of the late eighth century, yet formulated his lofty moralistic and deterrent ethic amidst a predatory society, and furthered the rationalism apparently most responsible for erosion of the social bond. Undoubtedly, ethical idealism advances in later prophetic writing, while moral thought becomes more elevated, and sinfulness is ever more severely censured. We find in the prophets and psalmists an ever more exalted conception of righteousness:

> I the Lord speak righteousness, I declare things that are right.[15]

> Righteousness shall go before him, and set us in the way of his steps.[16]

There is in their writing an ever fiercer anger and lamentation at the Hebrews' repudiation of righteousness through their sins:

> How is the faithful city become an harlot! It was full of judgement: righteousness lodged in it; but now murderers.[17]

> And he looked for judgement, but behold oppression; for righteousness, but behold a cry.[18]

And these are combined with increasingly dire threats of doom if this unrighteousness continues:

> And the destruction of the transgressors and sinners shall be together, and they that forsake the Lord shall be consumed.[19]

> If ye will not hearken to me, to walk in my law . . .
> then I will make the house like Shiloh, and will make
> this city a curse to all the nations of the earth.[20]

The later Hebrew poets oscillate between rapt expectation
that their people will come to serve righteousness, fury and
indignation at their present failure to do so, and promises of
fearful retribution on this account.

It does not follow, however, that the new moralism
brought, or reflected, a more humane ethical climate, and
certain features of it suggest the contrary. Righteousness –
which under the dispensation of the blessing had signified
soundness of being, the inner kernel of that fortunate state,[21]
but with the rise of holiness had more and more been seen
negatively as freedom from sin, and fear of the one holy god
– is now raised into a high abstract ideal that is synonymous
with perfection, and merges with the prophetic exaltation of
holiness itself: an ideal which is far above ordinary Israelites
and unattainable in its fullness by men, which is thus less
comprehensible and tangibly desirable than it once was, but
is nevertheless still supposed to produce just and right
conduct. More ominous still, it is the product of pure
ascendancy of the higher faculties, reflecting and strength-
ening commitment to a more absolute centralism, such as
disrupts the entirety that is the source of fellow feeling. No
wonder the prophet of righteousness is torn between love of
his high moral dream and wrath at his society's failure to
apply it.

We also find in the prophets much ferocious denunciation
of the folly and wickedness of the oppressive rich, apparently reflecting a situation where the greed and success of big
landowners has created an agrarian problem and political
unrest – one essentially similar in fact to that which led
Hesiod to indict the oppressive landlords of his day and to
exalt retributive justice. In particular, the prophets denounce
the ruling classes for their greedy accumulation of land and
property, riding roughshod over the needs of their humbler
compatriots:

Woe to them that join house to house, and lay field to field, till there be no place for the single field in the midst of the earth.[22]

Or,

And they covet fields, and take them by violence; and houses, and take them away; so they oppress a man and his house, even a man and his heritage.[23]

And they inveigh against their corruption and injustice:

They sold the righteous for silver, and the poor for a pair of shoes.[24]

Or,

They build up Zion with blood, and Jerusalem with iniquity. The heads thereof judge for reward, and the priests thereof teach for hire, and the prophets thereof divine for money: yet will they lean upon the Lord and say, Is not the Lord among us? none evil can come upon us.[25]

Yet again, this outpouring of the vials of wrath has qualities and deficiencies which do not suggest the coming of a kinder moral climate.

The promise of the imminent downfall of the great and powerful, it should be noticed, carries the old stress on bringing down the obnoxious mighty as an end in itself:

And he that is courageous among the mighty shall flee away naked in that day.[26]

Or once more,

Therefore shall the Lord, the Lord of hosts, send among his fat ones leanness; and under his glory he shall kindle a burning like the burning of a fire.[27]

Nor is there much if any sign in these prophets of real compassion for the poor and needy, who are referred to in perfunctorily general terms; their writing has a fanatical harshness barely compatible with kindness, and negative condemnation takes the place of a positive summons to social concern and justice. Moreover, the fundamental crime of the mercenary and despotic rich is the offence against the Holy and its god of their arrogance, which has turned a formerly faithful nation into a sinful one, that insults and detracts from divine holiness, rather than the wretchedness they have caused among the poor and weak.

We must not, then, identify the more complex and elevated moral thought of later prophecy, nor yet the exalted sacralism at its heart, with humane advance. Nor must we let blind progressivism cloud our judgement here. As H.W.F. Saggs justly observes,

> The assumption is commonly made that Mosaic Yahwism represented an advance over patriarchal religion; but, in so far as no attempt is made to substantiate this view by evidence, it appears to rest on no more than an evolutionary view of religious development. If one proposes to make value judgements over the matter, it is at least a theoretical possibility that the concept of deity attributed to the Mosaic period was a retrogression from that of the Patriarchs.*

If Mosaic Yahwism may represent a retrogression from patriarchal religious ideas, its later unfolding may equally well continue the process. And both these possibilities appear, when we look at the emergent humane pattern, to have been tragic realities.

---

* H.W.F. Saggs, *The Encounter with the Divine in Mesopotamia and Israel*, 1978, p. 36. He points most valuably to the possibility of retrogression, but does not really explore it, or offer any conclusion as to whether or not it occurred. His raising of the question is, I think, a telling example of the value of Sumerian material, as encouraging a fruitful scepticism towards received views of Hebrew religion.

3

Turning then to the ethical consequences of sacralism, the rise of holiness and its god seem to have darkened the humane scene. This effect is most pronounced in three main areas: the response to strangers, the treatment of enemy peoples and their territory, and finally the attitude to foreign nations, which will be considered in the next chapter. To begin with the first, in earlier times the stranger was not merely accepted, because he was re-enacting Israel's historic bondage in a strange land, but could be admitted into the presence of the Holy itself. This tolerance of aliens is remarkably persistent. As late as the days of Saul, Doeg the Edomite could dwell in an Israelite temple before the face of Yahweh, while under the early monarchy David could leave the Ark in the house of a Gittite worshipper of Edom, where it brought good rather than undergoing contamination.[28] One of the most moving stories in the Old Testament is that of Ruth, which may well incorporate early traditional material, although its author almost certainly belongs either to the time of the monarchy or to the post-exilic period – a tale whose organic provenance is shown by its many natural-istic images, such as the references to corn and sheaves,* by Boaz's blessing of Ruth because she has shown 'kindness', by its exceptional humane warmth, and not least by the total absence of the words 'holy' and 'holiness'. Its central point is that a foreign woman, a Moabite, is fully acceptable to God and Israel, and even worthy to become the ancestress of the great King David. But this relatively benign and outgoing response was not destined to prevail.

At length, a more rigorously conceived holiness must be strictly protected from the defiling and subtractive presence of the stranger, sometimes *per se,* and sometimes only if he has not been assimilated into Israel, by total conversion to its

---

* The story's organic ambience is unerringly registered by Keats, and distilled in his well remembered lines, 'Perhaps the self-same song that found a path/Through the sad heart of Ruth, when, sick for home,/She stood in tears amid the alien corn'.

religion. The stranger is prohibited from eating consecrated food:

> There shall no stranger eat of the holy thing.[29]

In accordance with the same principle, he is banned from even approaching the priests' domain, upon fear of death:

> And the stranger that cometh nigh shall be put to death.[30]

The unconverted stranger is likewise forbidden to enter the sanctuary:

> Thus saith the Lord God, No stranger, uncircumcised in heart, nor uncircumcised in flesh, shall enter into my sanctuary, of any stranger that is among the children of Israel.[31]

Hostility to the stranger reaches its apogee during the fifth century, with the purifying zeal of Nehemiah and Ezra. Nehemiah curses and smites certain Hebrews who have married aliens:

> In those days also saw I Jews that had married wives of Ashdod, of Ammon, and of Moab, and their children spake half in the speech of Ashdod, and could not speak in the Jews' language, but according to the language of each people. And I contended with them, and cursed them, and smote certain of them and plucked off their hair . . .[32]

Likewise, Ezra makes the people swear to put away all wives of foreign stock, and all children borne by them.[33] There is nothing surprising in the fact that militant exclusiveness thus prevailed, for it is a logical consequence of centralist holiness – which must enhance its isolation by making its select devotees ever more special and segregated, and banish from its presence every exception and threat to its pure ascendancy – and has the true dynamic of the ideal behind it;

although religious fear of syncretism is ever a precipitant and justification. These draconian prohibitions can only have ostracised that stranger in the midst whose hospitable reception had once been so admirable, a humane high water-mark in Hebrew life.

Upon the attitude to enemy peoples and their territory, the growing cult of the Holy had a more dire effect. For it soon created the savage concept of the holy war, with its attendant obligation to destroy unholy adversaries and everything that is theirs, a notion which became a lasting and influential feature of Hebrew thought. And it was freed from inhibition here by its centralist disruption of integrity, which prompts man to draw near to his fellows and care about their fate. In the era of the judges, those formidable early figures who combined the roles of holy man, prophet and warrior-leader, there emerged the dreadful ban of 'unholy' (*herem*). A foreign city pronounced unholy must be utterly destroyed, every living thing in it exterminated, and even its name blotted out, and never be revived lest it should contaminate. Destruction of an enemy city had apparently been regarded as a condition of divine support since Mosaic times:

> And Israel vowed a vow unto the Lord, and said, 'If thou wilt indeed deliver this people into my hand, then I will utterly destroy their cities.'[34]

Whether or not its full rigours are implied in the above passage, by the ban of *herem* this destructive commitment was made systematic and total. The most vivid and complete picture of the fate of an 'unholy' city is provided by the fearful account of the sack of Jericho:

> Joshua said unto the people, 'Shout; for the Lord hath given you the city. And the city shall be accursed, even it, and all that are therein, to the Lord' . . . And they utterly destroyed all that was in the city, both man and woman, young and old, and ox, and sheep, and ass,

with the edge of the sword . . . And Joshua adjured
them at that time, saying, 'Cursed be the man before
the Lord, that riseth up and buildeth this city Jericho:
he shall lay the foundation thereof in his first-born, and
in his youngest son shall he set up the gates of it.'[35]

To this day, the site of Jericho probably still bears the marks
of that scrupulous devastation.

The early prophets, who are governed by the vision
reflected in the Deuteronomic law, which plainly enunciates
the obligation to destroy an unholy city and all that is in it,
elaborate the doctrine of holy war into a detailed code of
destructive obligations. If a city is remote from Israel, 'very
far off from thee', it is only unholy in the second degree, so
that it suffices to 'smite every male thereof with the edge of
the sword', merely taking captive women, children and
cattle. But if it is an intrusively neighbouring one, and
destined to be appropriated by Israel, its whole population,
both human and animal, must be destroyed:

But in the cities of those people which Yahweh thy
God delivereth into thy possession, thou shall leave
alive nothing that hath breath.[36]

Only fruit-bearing trees are to be spared, apparently a relic
of ancient moderation and reflecting an enduring reverence
for trees. 'Are the trees of the field human beings that they
should be laid siege to by thee?'[37] In obedience to the
Deuteronomic conception of the holy war, when Jehoram
and Jehoshaphat go forth to reconquer the Moabites, Elisha
calls for the scorched-earth policy which it demands, even
ignoring the privileged status of trees:

Thou shalt reduce every fortified town and every
prominent city, and thou shalt cut down every good
tree and stop all fountains, and every good plot of land
you shall damage with stones.[38]

The forces of Israel and Judah obeyed Elisha to the letter:

> And they beat down the cities, and on every good piece
> of land cast every man his stone and filled it; and they
> stopped all the wells of water, and felled all the good
> trees . . .[39]

If Elisha is indifferent to the quality of mercy here, he is
faithful to the logic of his sacralist ideal, which demands that
whatever resists or threatens the Holy should be blotted
from the face of the earth. The extension of the aim of holy
war by later prophets, to embrace the destruction of whole
nations, we shall consider in a moment.

It is tempting to forget these accompaniments of growing
sacralism, the fierce intolerance of aliens, and boundless will
to annihilate the enemy and all that is his, and to feel that
they somehow flow from a primitive and untypical misapplication of the idea of the Holy, which ought not therefore to affect our view of the conception itself. For long, the
vested religious interest of the Christian and Jewish
communities of the world and the predominance of believers
in the field of biblical studies seem to have prevented truly
critical appraisal of the concept of holiness and its effects;
and there has therefore been a strong tendency to play down
these disturbing manifestations of it, as if they were only
minor and uncharacteristic blemishes upon the rise of
holiness.* Nothing could be further from the truth. In fact,
they represent the authentic and logical thrust of a cult of the
Holy, and we shall see later that the compulsions behind
them lie at the very centre of the Hebrew legacy. A clear
view here is not only vital for understanding Old Testament
psychology and ethics. Without this, we are ill positioned to
see the true impact of sacralism upon Western social history.

---

* However, the considerably more radical conclusions reached here find some
support, I think, in such studies as H. Fredriksson, *Jahwe als Krieger*, 1945, and
G. von Rad, *Der Heilige Krieg im alten Israel*, 1952.

5

HEBREW SACRALISM AND FOREIGN NATIONS

1

A sacralism harnessed to producing strength and potency, in order to win territory and greatness, was bound eventually to grow more ambitious, yielding to the flattering dream of world conquest. At the same time, the idea of the Holy One demanded that mankind should be one in acknowledging him: its absolute centralism would be incomplete if they did not. And thus was born Hebrew universalism, the prophetic hope of the world's surrender to Yahweh and Hebrew religion. We must not let its poetic vesture hide the overwhelmingly predominant fanatical harshness of the idea, or how little it holds of enlightened generosity. Essentially, it is a colossal power fantasy, with all the arrogant impatience that goes with these indulgences, blurred and softened a little at times by thin benevolist overtones, and the thought of peace. We shall look vainly in the universalist prophets for true tender concern for foreign peoples, such as the author of Jonah shows towards the people of Nineveh. Hebrew universalism also lacks the respect for subject peoples, and sensitivity to their needs and susceptibilities, the stress on trustworthy care and intent to benefit, and the endless patience in devising and implementing the best arrangements, which informed Roman imperialism and made possible its success, alongside much brutality and an ever-growing will to power. At best, no real interest is shown in how to translate ideological dream into practical reality, either through proper institutions or still more importantly through giving the new universal society a value to its beneficiaries, by making it psychologically attractive and creating a sense of family connection. Benign miracle, or else cataclysm, will bring surrender in an instant. At worst, the universalist vision is purely destructive: the total sway of Yahweh will come by eliminating other nations, or reducing them to irrelevant desolation. Hebrew universalism is a splendid, but barren and often cruel conception, which later did much to encourage the crusading excesses of medieval Christendom; although it also showed a little fertility by assisting richer visions of the unity of mankind, arising mainly from other causes, such as the emergent Roman belief that man is a citizen of the world.[1]

Hebrew universalist thinking was largely shaped by certain traditional and unfolding elements in earlier Hebrew thought: namely the concept and ideology of the holy war, the dreams of world conquest expressed in the royal psalms of Zion, the ancient prophetic obligation to curse other nations, and finally Yahweh's growing claim to eclipse and eventually oust all other national gods. The sacralist addiction to holy war in the Hebrews, requiring the destruction of the enemy and all that is his, and so obviously pointing to the extinction of foreign peoples and their deities, has just been reviewed. Later Hebrew prophecy never really freed itself from this sterile and destructive tradition. To begin then with prophetic malediction, this preoccupation of the later prophets is continuous with the earlier role of the prophet as sacral instrument of war, which has already been mentioned. One of the earliest forms of Hebrew prophecy, if not the earliest of all, was the oracle or curse against foreign powers, believed to be of semi-magical effect and to put enemies at no small disadvantage.[2] Maintaining this tradition, and including material apparently derived from it, a considerable portion of prophetic literature consists of curses against various nations, sometimes as oppressors of Israel, sometimes on any moral pretext to hand, sometimes for indeterminate pride against Yahweh, and sometimes for no apparent reason except antagonism and a will to magnify Israel's god and thus Israel itself. Arraigning Israel's neighbours on charges of utmost vagueness, Amos promises them unambiguous woe, and that the Lord will send fire, devour palaces and cut down inhabitants. Exultantly, Isaiah of Jerusalem announces the coming destruction of the Babylonians, that their children will be slaughtered before their eyes, their houses spoiled, their wives ravished, that their land will never be inhabited or even grazed again, but will become a habitat for wild beasts, owls and satyrs.[3] There will be similar calamities for Moab, for Tyre and Damascus, Assyria and Egypt, and even distant Ethiopia. Styling himself 'the prophet against the gentiles', Jeremiah curses virtually every nation within reach. With endless malicious bombast, he proclaims that the Babylonian Nebuchadnezzar will 'smite the land of Egypt' on Yahweh's behalf in a 'day of vengeance', that in Philistia 'all the inhabitants of the land shall howl', while Moab and the cities of Ammon, Hazor and Babylon, will suffer fates no less terrible. He calls too for a general pouring forth of fury upon all heathen nations who do not worship Yahweh:

> Pour out thy fury upon the heathen who know thee not,
> and upon the families that call not on thy name . . .[4]

In like vein and at great length, Ezekiel curses, not only Israel's traditional enemies – Ammon and Moab, Edom and Philistia – but also commercially sucessful Tyre, on the ground that she has rejoiced at the fall of Jerusalem, and even Israel's then potential ally Egypt, ostensibly to warn the Israelites against looking to Egypt for deliverance from Babylon.[5]

Hebrew universalism also builds upon the dream of world conquest set forth in the royal psalms of Zion, which envisage a defeat and subjection of the nations by the king, who will 'break them with a rod of iron' and 'dash them in pieces like a potter's vessel'.[6] This tradition of imaginings, in which realistic hope cannot readily be separated from mythopoeic adulation of the king, foresees a revolt of 'nations and peoples', who will hurl themselves against the lager of Zion, there to be scattered and destroyed by Yahweh in a terrifying apotheosis of self-exaltation and promotion of Israel to supreme worldly glory:

> There break he the flashing bow, the shield, the sword and the weapon . . . At thy rebuke, O God of Jacob, they lay stunned with their horses and chariots . . . He shall cut off the spirit of princes: he is terrible to the kings of the earth.[7]

Yahweh will then subject the defeated nations to the king: 'I shall give thee the heathen for thine inheritance, and the uttermost parts of the earth for thy possession.'[8] The dream of national aggrandisement could hardly go further.[9]

Finally, the universalist prophets were heirs of an expansionist drive built early, as we have seen, into the very conception of Israel's god, which demanded that he should either come to supersede foreign deities or annihilate the foreigners who believed in them. Even under the dispensation attributed to Mosaic times, it is part of his *raison d'être* to be mightier than other gods:

> Who is like unto thee, O Lord, among the Gods? Who is like thee, glorious in holiness, fearful in praises, doing wonders?[10]

Or again,

> Now I know that the Lord is greater than all the gods; for in the things wherein they dealt proudly he was above them.[11]

But this stage of belief in Yahweh's unique strength, which

lasts until the time of the ninth-century early prophets, still leaves living-space for other national deities. It can still admit the reality of other gods, conceding the validity of Moab's god Chemosh for the Moabites, and his activity and rights in Moabite territory,[12] and accepting that the Aramaean convert Naaman will worship his own people's god, Rimmon, when he returns to his own country.[13] But before long Yahweh is inexorably promoted to a position of king and judge over all other gods:

> For the Lord is a great god, and a great king above all gods.[14]

Or once more,

> God standeth in the congregation of the mighty; he judgeth among the gods.[15]

This more ambitious view inevitably soon culminates in the absolute monotheism of Deutero-Isaiah, who makes Yahweh declare: 'I am the Lord, there is none else, and beside me there is no God.'[16] As Yahweh thus gradually appropriates all divinity for himself, he has little choice but to become god of all the earth's peoples, except perhaps such as are rendered insignificant, or else to obliterate them.

Now all these formative influences upon burgeoning prophetic universalism have two elements in common: an over-mastering urge to aggrandise Israel's god, and the closely connected drive to extend the dominion of Israel. They also have two common negative elements: a general antagonism towards foreign peoples and an almost total lack of concern for their well-being and fulfilment. We would not expect a generous vision to spring from such parentage, and none did. To some extent, the major later prophets enlarged and reshaped the tradition in which they stood, showing considerable individuality and independence, but they could hardly redress such massive hostility to other nations.

2

The universalism of later Hebrew prophecy presents two main pictures of the future of the heathen. According to one, foreign nations subject themselves to the God of Israel and his people, either by becoming proselytes of her religion and deferring to her as a priestly elite or else by physically serving her as abject helots – unless, that is, they are destroyed or reduced to wretched insignificance for refusing to fall into line. According to the other, they do so by perishing. In both versions, the greatness of Yahweh and of Israel are paramount, foreign peoples being their unimportant instrument. We begin by considering the more benign conception of the two.

When we think of Hebrew universalism in its more beneficent aspect, our minds almost certainly turn first to the familiar and moving evocation of world unity and peace presented by Isaiah of Jerusalem (main author of Isaiah 1-39), whose call to be a prophet came *c.* 742-740, when Israelite-Judaean hegemony over Syria-Palestine was passing, and the rapid Assyrian penetration of the West beginning. Here Isaiah foresees a gathering of the nations around the temple in Zion, ruled by the god of Israel and obeying Israelite law:

And it shall come to pass in the last days that the mountain of the Lord's house shall be established in the top of the mountains, and shall be exalted above the hills; and all nations shall flow unto it. And many people shall go and say, Come ye, and let us go up to the mountain of the Lord, to the house of the God of Jacob; and he will teach us of his ways, and we will walk in his paths; for out of Zion shall go forth the law, and the word of the Lord from Jerusalem. And he shall judge among the nations, and shall rebuke many people: and they shall beat their swords into plough-shares, and their spears into pruning hooks: nation shall not lift up sword against nation, neither shall they learn war any more.[17]

To this should be added the similar lines from Micah, which are probably a displacement from it, foreseeing a time when peoples will flow into the house of Yahweh, on Zion his holy mountain, and law and judgement will go forth from it, so that 'nation shall not lift up a sword against nation', and every man shall sit unafraid under his own vine and ‖fig-tree.[18] Essentially it is a dream of peace, that old cherished function of the blessing, drawing upon the organic strand of thought which gave the Hebrews a deep feeling for peace, with a minimal idea of Israel as international benefactor. For Isaiah's vision is Israel-centred in the highest degree: the foreign peoples will stream into Zion, not into any other capital city or religious centre, submitting themselves to Hebrew beliefs and practices and abandoning their own, and making no contribution of any kind. If the familiar passage about the coming Messianic King, the 'Prince of Peace',[19] is by Isaiah of Jerusalem rather than a post-exilic addition, which seems probable but is a disputed point, it further shows how predominantly nationalistic is his conception of peace. For the ideal ruler will sit 'upon the throne of David', bringing government and peace 'upon his kingdom', which is not said to include foreigners.

Moreover, because it speaks to our hearts, we are apt to remember the passage just considered alone, fondly hoping that it is typical of Hebrew universalism. But the truth is very different. In reality, it is not even typical of Isaiah of Jerusalem.* We have already seen how avidly he curses foreign peoples, dealing out utter ruin to almost every heathen nation within reach. Isaiah of Jerusalem also

---

* Because Isaiah 1-39 has undergone expansion by later hands, it is not always possible to separate the original oracles; but there is little doubt that the thought of Isaiah of Jerusalem embraces broadly the elements ascribed to it in this chapter. The tendency today is to regard more material as authentically Isianic than was the case in the quite recent past. See John Mauchline, *Isaiah 1-39: Introduction and Commentary*, 1962, p. 17.

repeatedly returns to the thought of the Day of Yahweh, a great showing forth of his exaltation above all else, which holds little comfort for other nations, who will be summoned to hear their doom:

> For the indignation of Yahweh is upon all nations, and his fury upon all their armies: he hath utterly destroyed them, he hath delivered them to the slaughter.[20]

How thin is Isaiah of Jerusalem's international benevolism, how seldom in abeyance his will to aggrandisement, is also shown by his alternative imperialist picture of the nations' surrender to Israel. According to this vision, the nations who once oppressed Israel will become her captives and servants. 'And the house of Israel shall possess them in the land of the Lord for servants and handmaids: and they shall take them captive whose captives they were; and they shall rule over their oppressors.'[21]

What we may call 'benign universalism' – not because it was really benevolent, but to distinguish it from the more destructive form of universalism considered later – reaches its climacteric in the foreseen theocratic world-state of Deutero-Isaiah (author of Isaiah 40-55, whose activity belongs to the period 587-530), a vision conceived during the Exile in Babylon. According to Deutero-Isaiah, Yahweh will send his instrument Cyrus the Persian to conquer the Babylonians and set free the Israelites, who will triumphantly return to Jerusalem in a kind of second exodus and possession of the promised land. The conquests of Cyrus are effectively seen as achieved on behalf of Israel, or in place of Israel's conquest of the nations. There will follow a general surrender to Yahweh by the nations, who will turn to the god of Israel, forced to acknowledge his supremacy by this great exhibition of might:

> Turn to me, and be saved, all the ends of the earth. For
> I am God and there is no other . . . To me every knee
> shall bow, every tongue shall swear . . . In Yahweh
> shall triumph and glory all the offspring of Israel.[22]

How thinly disguised and improved a power fantasy is the
universalism of Deutero-Isaiah, how completely subordinated
to the glorification of Israel's god and his people, is clear
from the dominant note of divine and national triumph here.
It is shown too by Deutero-Isaiah's sublime contempt for
foreign nations:

> Lo, the nations are as a drop in the bucket, and are
> accounted as the small dust on the scales . . . All
> nations before thee are as nothing and vanity.[23]

Likewise, it is made plain when Deutero-Isaiah looks
forward exultantly to a Jerusalem from which all unconverted and unholy peoples are excluded:

> Put on thy beautiful garments, O Jerusalem, the holy
> city, for henceforth there shall no more come into thee
> the uncircumcised and the unclean.[24]

But above all, the religious imperialism of Deutero-Isaiah
is revealed as he discloses a boundless lust to subjugate
foreigners, when his picture of Israel as priestly ruler of the
nations shifts into a picture of her as their all-powerful task-
master, with foreign kings and queens serving Israel as abject
menials:

> And kings shall be thy nursing fathers, and their queens
> thy nursing mothers: they shall bow down to thee
> with their face toward the earth, and lick up the dust of
> thy feet.[25]

In this connection, it should be recalled that we meet the

same fantasy of utter subjugation again in the later and post-exilic Trito-Isaiah (main author of Isaiah 56-66, whose activity falls in the period between 537-455), very probably an adherent of the priestly hierarchy in power in restored Judah:

> And sons of strangers shall build up thy walls, and their kings shall minister unto thee . . . And strangers shall stand and feed your flocks, and the sons of the alien shall be your plowmen and your vine-dressers.[26]

Similar in spirit is the post exilic Micah's vision of the nations prostrating themselves in fear of Israel:

> The nations shall see and be ashamed of all their might: they shall lay their hands on their mouths, their ears shall be deaf. They shall lick the dusk like the serpent, like the crawling things of the earth. They shall come trembling out of their strongholds, they shall turn in dread to Yahweh our God, and they shall fear because of thee.[27]

This is not the language of benevolent internationalism, and neither is Deutero-Isaiah's description of bowing and foot-licking foreign kings and queens, in servitude to Israel. It is only the homeward-bound Israelites whom he envisages, drawing upon his considerable recessive pastoralism and feeling for the organic strand in Hebrew thought, as being gently tended by Yahweh:

> Say to the cities of Judah 'Behold your God', Behold Yahweh comes with might, and his arm shall rule for him: behold, his reward is with him and his recompense before him. He will feed his flock like a shepherd, he will gather the lambs in his arms; he will carry them in his bosom, and gently lead those that are with young.[28]

Eissfeldt has shown that not only the thought but even the diction of Deutero-Isaiah's vision is influenced by the just considered psalms of triumphant kingship, and particularly by Psalm 89, with its many images reminiscent of Deutero-Isaiah.[29] The broad continuity of Deutero-Isaiah's universalism with these fervid expansionist imaginings is plain enough. A false picture of Deutero-Isaiah, as a benevolent internationalist, has long been encouraged by a common misconstruction of his well remembered 'servant songs', and also to a lesser extent by mistranslation of one sentence in them (and of a variant of it); but I shall discuss these separately in a moment, since they have affected our view of 'benign' universalist prophecy as a whole.

In the post-exilic period, Zechariah and Haggai look forward to a religious triumph of Judah over the nations, accompanied by her political triumph. According to Haggai, the power of the gentile world will be destroyed – 'I will destroy the strength of the kingdom of the heathen'[30] – after which Yahweh's servant Zerubbabel will be installed as messianic ruler. When Yahweh has shaken the nations, 'the desire of the nations', namely religious and political obedience to a theocratic Hebrew ruler, will come to pass. The vision of Zechariah is very similar. The millenium will again begin with a pulverising of the might of heathen nations – 'I will shake my hand upon them, and they shall be a spoil to their servants.'[31] Then the messianic reign will be inaugurated, and many men and nations will join Israel: 'And many nations will be joined to the Lord in that day, and shall be my people';[32] 'And the Lord shall be King over all the earth: in that day shall there be one Lord and his name one'.[33] Those who will not come up to Jerusalem to worship the Lord will be plagued by loss of rain.[34] Zechariah's subjugatory attitude to foreign peoples is shown by his exultant picture of a Hebrew people glorified by all the appropriated wealth and possessions of the heathen: 'And the wealth of all the heathen round about shall be gathered together, gold and silver, and apparel, in great abundance.'[35] Zechariah is not the only universalist prophet who dreams thus of plundering the world to adorn Jerusalem. Trito-Isaiah also looks forward to the same gratifying prospect: '. . . ye shall eat the riches of the gentiles, and in their glory shall ye boast yourselves.'[36]

3

A grotesquely idealised picture of the internationalism of the prophets, ascribing to them a non-existent grand catholicity, has long been furthered by misinterpretation of the 'servant songs' in Deutero-Isaiah, and in smaller measure by misleading translation of a particular sentence in them (and of a variant of it). H.M. Orlinsky has shown this,[37] and with such brilliance and meticulous thoroughness that it is best here simply to summarise his analysis and conclusions. The 'servant songs'[38] have often been held to present the people of Israel as 'Suffering Servant', atoning vicariously, through its adversities, for the sins of the nations. We must therefore consider Orlinsky's case against this view in some detail. He makes four main objections, each weighty in itself, and in combination I think fatal, which I shall first enumerate briefly, before presenting them more fully. First, the so-called 'Suffering Servant' must, when we look closely at the text, be seen as an individual rather than the people of Israel. Second, the most essential element in the idea of vicariousness – that the guilty go unpunished – is completely missing from the passages concerned, from the thought of Deutero-Isaiah, and from the Old Testament as a whole. Third, the idea of Israel's suffering innocently, on behalf of non-Israelites, is flatly at odds with all Old Testament thinking in this area, including that of Deutero-Isaiah. Last, the technical term 'Suffering Servant' does not occur in the Old Testament, but is a post-biblical phenomenon, a product of Christianity in the period subsequent to the death of Jesus.

The servant of Yahweh must be an individual, because

repeated use is made of expressions which make perfect
sense if applied to a particular speaker, and virtually none if
applied to the people of Israel. For instance, the statements
'He hath made my mouth like a sharp sword, he made me a
polished arrow'[39] and 'He will not cry out or raise his voice
and cause it to be heard in the open'[40] are fully intelligible if
they refer to an individual spokesman, but incomprehensible
when construed as referring to Israel. It is as a person-
ification of the unpopular and much-suffering prophet and
his role that the servant is best understood. The prophet
does indeed suffer, for his perennial message of rebuke
ensures that – it can entail abuse, or jail, or even death – and
the people have repented, and enjoyed the fruits of repent-
ance, because he has thus suffered. He bears a double load of
suffering, that which he shares with his people in consequence of national sin and that associated with his own
painful mission. But, if the people had not sinned, he would
not need to suffer in either way. It is in this sense only that
Isaiah asserts, 'The chastisement of our welfare was upon
him, and through his stripes we were healed . . . and
Yahweh caused to fall on him the guilt of us all.'[41]

The one stumbling-block for this otherwise overwhelmingly convincing view is Isaiah 49, 3, where the servant of
Yahweh is addressed as 'Israel'. However, Orlinsky argues
powerfully that the word *yisra'el* is a secondary intrusion
here, partly because grievous 'contextual difficulties' arise if
its presence is genuine, but also because it is used here in a
different manner from that of its other forty-two occur-
rences in Deutero-Isaiah. One Hebrew manuscript (Kenn 96)
omits the word *yisra'el* here. *La Sainte Bible* places it within
parentheses, and adds as a note, 'Cette precision, difficile-
ment compatible avec les vv. 5-6, cf. 42, 1ff., est sans doute
une glose.' The matter of incompatibility is, I think, crucial.
If we accept *yisra'el* as genuine here, we render the 'servant
songs' as a whole unintelligible. It is this which leads von
Rad likewise to conclude that the 'collective interpretation of
the servant raises insuperable difficulties'.[42] He also points

out that it is incompatible with Deutero-Isaiah's plain assertion that the servant has a mission *to* Israel,[43] and that the servant's innocence and complete self-surrender to Yahweh are not remotely to be found in the people of Israel at large.[44]

As regards the claim that Israel suffers vicariously for the nations' sins, the essence of vicariousness is that the culpable wicked go unpunished, because the substitute victim has paid their penalty. But there is no suggestion in Deutero-Isaiah, let alone elsewhere in the Old Testament, that foreign peoples, or Israel itself, have gone unpunished. Indeed, the theme of their fearful punishment is one of the most persistent in the Old Testament, while Israel has just undergone, through the Exile, its greatest disaster since the captivity in Egypt – a catastrophe which Deutero-Isaiah himself sees as divine retribution for the nation's sins. The idea of Israel as sacrificial substitute-victim, on behalf of other nations, is completely contrary to the subjugatory, and almost totally unaltruistic, attitude towards them found throughout the Old Testament, and not least in Deutero-Isaiah. In Orlinsky's pointed words, 'It is unheard of in the Bible that Israel, God's treasured people, his partner in the covenant, should suffer innocently for any non-Israelite peoples.'[45] As for the idea of the so-called 'Suffering Servant', there is no trace in the Old Testament of this technical term. It was only after vicarious suffering came to be associated with Jesus that this concept was read back into the Old Testament passages most favourable for such interpretation, namely the 'servant songs' of Deutero-Isaiah. In short, the idea of the 'Suffering Servant' is 'a theological and scholarly fiction'. When we approach the 'servant songs' afresh, freed by Orlinsky's arguments from a readiness to read into them post-biblical ideas, the oft-expressed view that they present Israel as vicarious sufferer on behalf of the nations – in fact a forerunner of Christ, seen under the aspect of the doctrine of the Atonement - seems, I think, quite unsustainable, and even preposterous. Nevertheless, this interpretation of the 'servant songs' must have swayed many of us towards an uncritical and falsely rosy picture of Deutero-Isaiah's universalism, and that of the 'benign' universalist prophets more generally, encouraging us to think of them in misleadingly internationalist terms.

There are also certain single sayings which have been likewise miscontrued, to give a false picture of the prophets as benevolent internationalists. The most important of these is Deutero-Isaiah's sentence, 'I will make thee (the servant of Yahweh) a covenant of people, a light of nations.'[46] Orlinsky shows that 'covenant of people' is best understood as 'a consolidation of people' (i.e. the Hebrew people); and that 'a light of nations' (misleadingly translated both in the Authorised Version and the Revised Standard Version as 'a light *to* the Gentiles', which gives a sense of movement towards and intent to benefit) probably signifies a dazzling and over-aweing of the nations by Israel's God-given restoration to her homeland, rather than a fulfilling of their unsatisfied religious aspirations. In other words, Deutero-Isaiah's intention here is indeed *universalist*, but not in any real sense *internationalist*. A variant of the sentence just considered runs 'I will make thee a light of nations, that thou mayest be my salvation unto the end of the earth.'[47] Orlinsky argues convincingly that the last phrase signifies a gathering of dispersed Israelites, such as Deutero-Isaiah envisages when he writes elsewhere:

> I will bring thy seed from the east and gather thee from the west; I will say to the north, Give up; and to the south, Keep not back: bring my sons from far, and my daughters from the ends of the earth.[48]

This interpretation is the more persuasive because the words immediately preceeding the sentence under review – 'that thou shouldest be my servant to raise up the tribes of Jacob, and to restore the preserved of Israel' – plainly refer to a restoration of scattered Hebrews. All this being so, and in view of the confusing post-biblical overtones of 'salvation', a more satisfactory translation is 'saving victory'. There are a few other more minor sentences of other prophets – particularly Mal. 2, 10, 'Have we not all one father? Has not Yahweh created us?' (referring exclusively to Judah, and rebuking sacerdotal elements for arrogance) – which, sometimes wrenched completely out of context, have been similarly misinterpreted in internationalist terms, and which the reader will find fully discussed by Orlinsky.[49] Finally, it should be remembered here that this small group of sayings is quantitatively eclipsed by literally hundreds of contrary ones – from Genesis to the prophets – which quite unambiguously assert, or reflect, the relationship of Yahweh and Israel as purely nationalistic.

4

But other prophets felt, logically enough, that the glory of the holy Yahweh and Israel would be best served by a more drastic and magnificent apotheosis still, namely the extermination of heathen peoples, in a final holy war to end all holy wars, the more ruthless and comprehensive for being realised only in fantasy – an attitude which we may call 'destructive universalism'. The escalating cult of the Holy culminates, quite naturally, in the prophetic proclamation that entire nations must and will be annihilated. The seventh-century Zephaniah foresees a storm of divine destruction which will sweep over the accursed heathen nations:

> Therefore wait ye upon me, saith the Lord, until the day that I rise up to the prey: for my determination is to gather the nations, that I may assemble the kingdoms to pour upon them mine indignation, even all my fierce anger: for all the earth shall be devoured with the fire of my jealousy.[50]

To this group of destructive sayings, should be added Isaiah of Jerusalem's already considered words:

For the indignation of Yahweh is upon all nations, and
his fury upon all their armies: he hath utterly destroyed
them, he hath delivered them to the slaughter.[51]

Nahum, who describes the downfall of Nineveh, capital of
Assyria, in 612 BC, pronounces the avenging wrath of
Yahweh upon the oppressive and idolatrous city: 'He that
dasheth in pieces'[52] will utterly obliterate Nineveh. 'Woe to
the bloody city . . . And it shall come to pass that all that
look upon thee shall flee from thee, and say, Nineveh is laid
waste.'[53] The fruit of the destruction of Nineveh will be
peace to Israel: '. . . behold upon the mountains the feet of
him that bringeth good tidings, that publisheth peace!'[54] With
our incorrigible tendency to read and remember the Old
Testament selectively, harbouring in our minds just what is
most sympathetic, we are liable to recall only these words of
the savage prophet, along with a few similar prophetic
sayings. If so, we are not the first to react thus: a culling of
such excerpts, woven into the unquestioning hearts of
generations by beautiful music, is to be found in Handel's
Messiah. The hope that Nineveh will repent, turning to
Israel's god and thus averting her destruction, which we saw
to have been so tenderly entertained by the author of Jonah,
with his exceptional responsiveness to the organic underside of
the Hebrew tradition, does not even occur to the sacralist
Nahum. Because the passages concerned are uncongenial, and
we therefore tend to consign them to oblivion, we are apt also
to forget what an insistent theme in Hebrew prophecy is the
destruction of the nations.

But the last annihilation of the heathen is conjured up in its
most extreme form, and with the most unashamed dwelling
upon detail, in the sacralist prophet *par excellence,* the sixth-
century Ezekiel, whose thought spans the period just before
the fall of Judah in 587, and also extends into that of the
Exile. It is the lofty Ezekiel – the prophet who not only lifts
the holy god high in transcendent majesty but views Israel as
the 'holy flock' which will serve the Lord in his

'holy mountain', and foresees a temple with 'holy chambers' where the priests who approach the lord will eat 'the most holy things' – who gives us the most loving, the most dreadful picture of the destruction of unholy nations. Ezekiel looks forward to a last slaughter of invading heathen peoples from afar, made to seem monstrous and dispensable by the collective name of 'Gog'. After Israel has repossessed Canaan, destroying the occupying or threatening Edomites and making them and their cities 'perpetual desolations', Yahweh will unwittingly lure Gog to besiege Zion's sacred citadel, to his own destruction and Yahweh's greater glory. Ezekiel describes how Yahweh will inspire the foreign hosts with supernatural panic, leading to mutual destruction. Then he will pour down final terrors upon them as a final theophany, a vindication of his greatness and holiness before all the world:

> And I will plead against him with pestilence and with blood; and I will rain upon him, and upon his bands, and upon the many people that are with him, an overflowing rain, and great hailstones, fire and brimstone. Thus will I *magnify myself and sanctify myself;* and I will be known in the eyes of many nations, and they shall know that I am the Lord.[55]

Ezekiel finds this climax of history so enthralling that he repeats himself, telling again how the unholy invaders 'shall fall upon the mountains of Israel', so that Yahweh will make his 'holy name known' in the midst of his people, and compel the heathen to know that 'I am the Lord, the Holy One in Israel'.[56]

For Ezekiel, this massacre of foreigners is a necessary blazoning forth of holiness, and a fulfilment of its demands, so much so that he drives home the point four times in slightly different words.[57] Indeed, Ezekiel is so obsessed with his foreign hordes, and their fate, that he goes on ghoulishly to embroider his vision, telling how Yahweh will summon the birds and beasts to devour the fallen:

Thus saith the Lord God; Speak unto every feathered fowl, and to every beast of the field, Assemble yourselves, and come; gather yourselves on every side to my sacrifice that I do sacrifice to you, even a great sacrifice upon the mountains of Israel, that ye may eat flesh and drink blood. Ye shall eat the flesh of the mighty, and drink the blood of the princes of the earth . . .[58]

If this scene of carnage emphatically does not reflect the view that God blesses all the families of the earth, it represents an authentic climax of belief in him as holy. It also finally disposes of an illusion already mentioned – namely that holy war, and the urge utterly to destroy the unholy, spring from a primitive and untypical misapplication of the concept of the Holy.

In this culminating vision of sacralist universalism, in its destructive form, even if whole national communities are dissidents, an exception and risk to the total supremacy of holiness and its god, they must be annihilated. There is a fierce logic in this consummation of sacralism. It presents a deity who fully satisfies the principles of the sacralist vision: a sovereign god in isolated majesty, not open to affront by the existence of nations other than the one he has chosen, and segregated to acknowledge his holiness, who empowers his people to limitless aggrandisement. If this suggests a radical connection between sacralism and savagery, there is nothing really surprising here. Sacralism was yoked from the first, as we have seen, to a ruthless and boundlessly expansionist warrior-god, in accordance with its purpose of conferring centralist strength in the interest of territorial conquest. If limited holiness demands holy war, fully developed holiness licenses, nay demands, holy genocide. As Israel sought to become a holier nation, it grew ever more prone to fanatical extremism, which came at length to know no limit. Historic factors, such as the Exile, may have assisted and precipitated this dire finale; but it is only intelligible, particularly in a people so well able to conserve where it has the will, as stemming inevitably from the evolution of sacralist centralism. To anticipate the next stage of our study, this goes far to explain why, when the Hebrew centralist concept of a holy god and the Greek one of sovereign reason finally united in the fourth-century fusion of Judaeo-Christian and Hellenic thought, the result was not a more humane Europe, still less a great expansion of the humanitarian spirit. Together with the ferocious imperialism we have found in the less fanatical universalist prophets, it also helps us to see why the pursuit of other-worldly sanctity in both the patristic age and the Middle Ages was so constantly and unstrainfully accompanied by a consuming will to power.

PART TWO

THE HISTORIC SEQUEL

6

HOLINESS AND THE HUMANE RESPONSE IN THE AGE OF THE FATHERS - I

1

Our next task is to examine the humane response of the patristic era. But first we should take note of the small band of patristic men and women who, like their counterparts in all ages, showed exceptional compassion or dedication to charitable activity, and who therefore were and often are called 'holy', or else 'saints'. For we must guard from the outset against a misunderstanding that readily arises from this classification. When such people were described as holy (or saints), the last thing meant was that the concept of the Holy was known to have been their psychic dominant. This would have been formidably difficult to establish in any case, and certainly no one tried to do so. Rather, the epithet 'holy' was invoked when a Christian, possibly a layman but preferably a cleric, showed an extraordinary intensity of devotional life, or zeal on behalf of the Church, or radiancy of goodness, or heroic obedience to the gospel; so that he or she lent themselves to a sacralist view of virtue, which sees it as primarily located in *special and isolated centres*. The distinguishing mark of the 'holy' was that they seemed to be peculiarly vouchsafed by the centralist and holy god, because apparently segregated from the great multitude of ordinary good men and women, presenting themselves as human counterparts of holy places and objects.

Although the standard grew ever more stringent, so as not to debase the currency, any Christian who for almost any reason made the requisite mark, displayed the needful religious or moral or political star quality, was eligible for the badge of holiness. It could be given alike to the inhumane but devotionally and theologically amazing Augustine, to the cantankerous Wilfred, who fought so hard and effectively for the interests of the Church, or to the gentle Cuthbert, who communed with seals. Hence, when this badge is accorded to the outstandingly caring or charitable, it is not really claimed that the idea of the Holy ruled their mental life, although we are encouraged to assume that. Even if they reached their compassion through exceptional *resistance* to the notion, and natural generosity stemming from a rich organic endowment, fed by corresponding responsiveness to nature and the organic stratum in the Old Testament and gospels themselves – but perhaps sometimes drawing upon holiness too, recessively and selectively, for an added edge of discipline and dedication – they still qualify as holy, so long as their lives and works make them seem isolated moral centres. In this context, the word 'holy' is not a psychological description but a partisan accolade.

More than anything else, I believe, this subtle source of confusion has tended to fog the whole issue of sacralism, and its humane consequences. Because of it, we feel unable to question the concept of the Holy, without denigrating by implication the honourable band of 'holy' men and women. It is also an intellectual step which makes holiness seem indubitably the fount of charitable concern, whereas it was argued earlier that the true thrust of a cult of holiness is towards aggrandisement and inhumanity. Thus, the so-called 'holy' men and women of the patristic era and the Middle Ages, or indeed of other times, are beside the point here, since they establish nothing beyond the recurrence of exceptional individuals, and the sacralist mind's perennial need and will to sanctify. Therefore, however worthy of respect in themselves, we should forget them as a class now, along with the hopeless task of identifying their various psychic priorities, and concentrate instead on the pertinent and possible one: that of discovering how the humane response fared generally in the centuries when sacralism held sway, which may shed some light upon its nature and effects. To the concept of the Holy itself, on the other hand, we must soon return.

2

An optimistic view of the humane response in the patristic period, or indeed the medieval, is unlikely to survive even brief reflection upon their history. The grim records of actual brutality and oppression in both periods are best recalled simultaneously, for they are writ plain and need not detain us long. We remember here the early fathers' arrogant and enthusiastic belief in exclusive salvation, their proud certainty that the whole pagan world was destined for hell, so powerfully summed up in Origen's famous saying, 'Without this house, that is without the Church, no-one is saved', or the unanimous view of the early church, systematically justified by Augustine,* that all infants who died unbaptised were, notwithstanding their Saviour's well attested special love for them, excluded from heaven; or how successive Councils of the Church anathematised the pathetic practices by which mothers often persuaded themselves that their children might nevertheless be received into paradise. We remember too the dreadful history of religious persecution, rife from the Conversion of Constantine onwards, once more zealously supported by Augustine† and

---

* For an account of Augustine's sentiments on Infant Baptism, see W. Wall, *History of Infant Baptism*, 1705, vol. 2, pp. 192-206. Few sharper pictures of inhumanity, justified by high-minded reasoning, will readily be found, than on these unduly neglected pages.

† See *Retractions*, Bk II, ch. 5, *Epistolae* XCIII (or XCVIII in some editions), CXXVII, CXXXV, *Contra Gaudentium*, ch. 25, and elsewhere in his writings. On account of the zeal with which Augustine joined the late Roman emperors, in the persecution of pagans and heretics, he has been called *le prince et patriarche des persécuteurs*.

later by Aquinas‡, instigated by the most lofty and dedicated minds, and apparently enjoying the broad support of their communities. Again, we remind ourselves of those terrible coercive wars of religion, the Crusades, with their unreckonable tolls of devastation and suffering. Or, once more, we call to mind the meagre toleration accorded at best to the Jewish community by medieval Christendom, an attitude which Aquinas at length authoritatively defines and squares with theology, by justifying their despoliation, but insisting on their right to live:

> Because of their sins (of unbelief), they are subject to perpetual servitude, and their goods are at the disposition of the ruler; only he must not take from them so much that they are deprived the means of life.[1]

As we think of these things, we realise how unlikely it is that the patristic or medieval periods were notable for humane compassion. And our sadness at this improbability grows stronger as we reflect that those concerned were not barbarians or primitives, but highly intelligent and sensitive men, inhabitants of a great civilisation, in pursuit of a gleaming ideal vision.

3

As for the more complex matter of positive humane progress in the patristic era, its record here confirms and extends this sorry first impression. Let us first consider the fathers' response to the most crying social evil of their day, the institution of slavery, that most dreadful oppression and denial of basic rights, of which Jefferson, even though he was himself a slave-owner, wrote with profound realism and disquiet,

‡ 'Since counterfeiters are justly killed by princes as enemies to the common good, so heretics also deserve the same punishment' (*Summa Theologiae*, II, 2, 11, 3).

The whole commerce between master and slave is a perpetual exercise of the most boisterous passions, the most unremitting despotism on the one part, the most degrading submission on the other. The man (the master) must be a prodigy who can maintain his manners and morals undepraved by such circumstances.[2]

The attitude of the fathers to this iniquity rests mainly on two beliefs, coexisting in uneasy partnership: first, that God does not in principle approve of the custom, having originally intended men to live in brotherly equality, as indeed they once did in a first paradisial state from which they have since fallen; but secondly, that it is now, *faute de mieux*, part of his scheme for the human race, being an inevitable expression of man's bondage to sin, a needful punishment for this self-inflicted condition, and a means of its disciplinary correction.

Now let us recall the fathers' actual words and arguments on the subject. In the course of a classic statement of the church's theory of the origin and rationale of slavery, Augustine sets forth the ·supposed penal rightness and efficacy of the institution:

The first cause of slavery is sin, by which man is subject to man by the bonds of his condition; which servitude does not come about, except by the judgement of God, with whom is no wickedness, and who knows how to distribute various penalties, according to the merits of offenders.[3]

Ambrose, who insists that slavery to sin is the overriding evil, is tirelessly ingenious in devising justifications of actual slavery. For a weak and foolish man to be a slave, he maintains, is really for his good. 'He who cannot govern and control himself ought to be in subjection to one who is more prudent . . . It is as a blessing therefore that such a state of servitude is given.'[4] Or again, 'Folly is so much worse than slavery, that slavery may be reckoned as a remedy for it.'[5] According to Ambrose, slavery is only a minor evil, because it affects only the body, leaving the mind free: 'the flesh may be enslaved, but the mind is free'.[6] Lastly, slavery gives the slave a unique opportunity to show the superiority of higher freedom, by leading a life of unservile virtue in servile circumstances:

> God allotted mastery . . . that they might learn that many slaves are freer than their masters, if those placed in servitude consider to abstain from servile deeds. For all sin is slavery, innocence is liberty.[7]

'The crucial thing is, not that station should dignify character, but that character should dignify situation.'[8] Later, a more complacent response still is expressed in Isodore of Seville's cold dictum, 'Subject slavery is better than exalted freedom.'[9]

This whole body of teaching, explaining and justifying slavery, placed the now enormous authority of the church squarely behind the worst of all forms of human exploitation. It does not seem to have troubled the fathers that this supposedly necessary and remedial state, with its extreme distresses, was unevenly distributed among mankind, or that the slave-owning class was bereft of its imputed saving benefits. Surely, even when we have allowed for the blinkering power of the *Zeitgeist*, the difficulty of questioning what one's society assumes to be right and inevitable, this fact, and the attitudes which led to it, indict the humanity of the fourth-century fathers.

As we next turn to the patristic humane contribution more generally, it is best to concentrate upon the fourth and early fifth centuries, the time when the degree of reserve towards Hellenic speculation hitherto shown by the Christian thinkers of the 'Latin' West is finally overcome; when Augustine sets the final seal upon the church's long growing *rapprochement* with Greek intellectualist metaphysics and

ethics; when Christians, ceasing to be a harassed and per-
secuted minority mainly drawn from the humblest classes,
and driven to band together in mutual support by the
pressures of this situation alone, become a large and socially
diverse group enjoying the support of the state, and thus
capable of influencing the community at large; and when the
main institutions of medieval Christendom are founded and
decisively shaped. We might therefore naively expect that the
church, which had a quite impressive earlier record of
charitable works,* now enjoying the full benefits both of the
Sermon on the Mount and Greek thought, would at this
point enter into its own, humanising and morally revitalising
the whole of its society. It was not to be.

The moral anticlimax which in fact followed is well
summed up by A.H.M. Jones, in his monumental *The Later
Roman Empire*:

> There were many good Christians who were charitable
> to the poor, but many more who abused their wealth
> and position to exploit their necessities, lending them
> money at usurious rate of interest, enslaving them when
> they were starving, juggling with the assessments to
> throw on them more than their due of taxation, extort-
> ing from them extra perquisites beyond their lawful rent,
> and cheating them by the use of false measures. It is
> difficult to assess whether in these matters the general
> level of morals was lower than it had been under the
> pagan empire, *but it seems to have been no higher.*†

* These included alms in general, the support of widows and orphans, the support of
the sick, the infirm and the disabled, and the care of prisoners and workers
languishing in the mines. See Chapter 4 on 'The Gospel of Love and Charity', in
Harnack, op. cit.

† A.H.M. Jones, *The Later Roman Empire; A Social, Economic and Administrative
Survey*, 1964, vol. 2, p.978. The italics are mine. Jones also points out that this broad
moral pattern, as well as being unequivocally set forth by Servian (a not altogether
reliable witness) in his *de Gubanatore Dei*, is amply borne out by much factual
evidence, in the Codes, in the canons of the Councils, in the letters of laymen and
ecclesiastics, in the speeches of Libianus and the sermons of bishops, and in the
papyri.

He goes on to darken the picture considerably:

> In some aspects of morals, it is possible to trace a decline. The codes give a strong indication that brutality increased.[10]

And he then points, with a perplexed surprise which we can only share, to the central problem for an appraisal of fourth-century Christianity, the fact that its triumph appears not to have led to moral advance, and to have been followed in many areas by moral decline:

> It is strange that, during a period when Christianity, from being the religion of a small minority, came to embrace practically all the citizens of the empire, the general standards of conduct should have remained in general static, and in some respects have sunk.[11]

This was an age when a formidable systematic coherence, intellectual and instutional, and a profoundly impressive loftiness of outlook, both largely stemming from the Greek inheritance, helped to create new social forms of great historic importance: the monastery, the hierarchy of the Christian church, the idea of Christian empire. Yet there seems to have been no correspondent flowering of loving kindness or sensitive concern for the unfortunate, but rather a retreat from the levels so far attained.

How did this come about, when the church had at its disposal a most powerful, even intimidating system of religious thought and practice, by which to commend and enforce almost anything that it profoundly wanted to achieve? Certainly, it was not for lack of financial resources, since we learn that the episcopate cost even more than the injuriously expensive imperial bureaucracy, while the church's salary bill well exceeded that of the empire.[12] It may be said, of course, and often has been said, that this was the inevitable price of respectability, a lowering of standards necessitated, or at least made too likely not to happen, by the conversion of Constantine. But, although this may indeed have been a contributory factor, as a fundamental explanation it is unconvincing. It cannot really have been beyond the persuasive resources of the church substantially to communicate even to quite affluent Romans, if it had passionately wanted to, the infinitely rich principle of love of one's neighbour. Surely, the most likely fundamental cause is one which seems nearly always to be at work when things that might well have been done in fact are not: that the main thrust of energy and interest was directed elsewhere. Periodically, of course, the fathers commended charity and compassion in their writings, as a recessive and somewhat routine element in their teaching, in company with other virtuous states of mind, such as patience and perseverance.[13] But the crux of the matter remains that they systematically promulgated views which are the negation of ·kindness, and omitted to throw their formidable personalities and great power over the minds of men into the task of building a more compassionate society.

4

Why then did the Christian fathers, heirs to a gospel of love and the parable of the Good Samaritan, embrace grievous inhumanities like the consignment of most of mankind to hell, including unbaptised infants? Why did they not only condone slavery but actually support it by subtle theological arguments? Why did moral standards not rise with the triumph of Christianity, but even decline in some areas? And, at the root of all these questions, what were the aims which enjoyed the overriding allegiance of leading fourth-century Christians, thus channelling their energies and passions, at the expense of humanity and moral concern?

In the first place, there was in the fathers a deep-seated will to transfer moral issues from the factual and human level to the theological. This was notably so, for instance, as regards their attitude towards the evil of poverty, that devastating plight of which Johnson so truthfully and eloquently writes:

> In the prospect of poverty, there is nothing but gloom and melancholy; the mind and body suffer together; its miseries bring no alleviation; it is a state in which every virtue is observed, and in which no conduct can avoid reproach; a state in which cheerfulness is insensibility, and dejection sullenness, of which the hardships are without honour, and the labours without reward.[14]

Even in the Old Testament, there had been some acknowledgement, as we saw earlier, of the duty to alleviate poverty; for the psalmist writes, 'Blessed is he that considereth the poor.'[15] Yet when Ambrose ponders this text, he is prompted to alter its meaning and thrust, by construing it in terms of Christ's self-impoverishment, in foregoing the riches of divinity, to take upon himself the poverty of our human state:

> Blessed is he who is mindful of the indigence and poverty *of Christ*, he who, from being rich, has become poor for us: rich in his kingdom, yet poor in our flesh . . . He has suffered, not in his riches, but in our poverty.[16]

Likewise, Augustine declares that 'to be mindful of the poor and indigent' is above all to have faith, and maintain a precise trust in the mystery of the Incarnation, of that poor one *par excellence* who was the son of God made man.[17] He adds as an afterthought, it should in fairness be added, that men ought to 'consider also the poor and needy', as a means of understanding Christ. The manifest effect of this reinterpretation is to deflect these theologians from the problem of *actual* poverty towards the ideal of *religious* poverty, of

identification with the voluntary self-pauperising of Christ,
as effected through his Incarnation. Thus, there is conspicuously missing in their writings the Johnsonian note of
outrage at the humiliating sufferings of the poor, and his
appalled awareness of their concrete distresses. Through the
same moral emigration from the earthly to the heavenly
plane, the fourth-century fathers were apparently so
obsessed with *theological* enslavement – the overriding evil,
as they saw it, of man's bondage to sin – that they accepted
the terrible slavery of fact.

Next, the fathers inherited from early Christianity a
commitment, owing much to Hellenic influence, to sever-
ance from this life in the interest of a future one, and a
tendency to make this aim the main principle sustaining
morality and self-control, at the expense of charitable
concern for present human needs and distresses. Even Paul
had taught, 'Set your affection on things above, not on
things on the earth.'[18] 'May Grace come, and this world pass
away' had likewise long been the prayer of the church at
every service.[19] 'The present and the future age are enemies,'
the late-second-century Clement had written.[20] And he had
continued:

> We cannot, therefore, be friends of both; we must
> part with the one and embrace the other. We judge it
> better to hate the things that are here, because they are
> small and transient and corruptible, and to love the
> things that are yonder, for they are good and
> incorruptible.

This world-abandoning response had since become more
intense and universal, gathering new momentum in the third
century, affecting Christians and pagans alike, and reflecting
the impact of an age of anxiety and political disturbance
upon a mainly Hellenic readiness to resort to programmes of
withdrawal and ascent – essentially the same readiness that
had earlier made many Greeks turn to the world-abandoning

cults of Pythagoreanism and Orphism.[21] And at this point we must pause briefly to consider that Greek addiction to mysticism, since it is acutely relevant for understanding patristic obsession with the life to come.

5

The Greeks show from the sixth century onwards a strong propensity to mystical cults, of a type essentially peculiar to the Greek world,[22] whose common feature is the supposed conferring of special privileges, particularly in the next life. First, there are the mysteries of Eleusis, of whose content we know very little indeed, since both the literary and iconographical sources respect their secrets. They had a strong connection with the fertility myth of Demeter and her daughter Kore-Persephone, consisted of ritual acts and spectacle, 'things done' and 'things seen', and were believed to transform the lot of the initiate in this life, but especially in the next. 'For him alone there will be life down there,' a Sophoclean fragment declares of him who has been initiated.[23] The Eleusinian mysteries seem mainly to have offered an unexacting means of insurance to those preoccupied with their future state. Next, we have the austere spirituality of the Pythagoreans: the surviving evidence indicates that they believed the soul to be a fallen divinity, confined within the body as a tomb, fated to a cycle of reincarnation as man, animal or plant, unless it wins release by cultivating purity. The life and teaching of Pythagoras are mostly lost to us, while Pythagoreanism's debt to, and degree of overlap with, Orphism remain unsolved problems.

Finally, all this futuristic striving is consummated in the powerful Orphic movement, capable of influencing such original minds as Pindar and Empedocles and Plato, and whose growth was only briefly arrested by the mood of euphoria and worldliness following the defeat of the Persians, soon reasserting itself with new vigour. Orphism represents the quintessence of life-denial. The central doctrine of Orphism was that the soul is an alien and prisoner within the body, and in this earthly life, these incarcerating forms being contrary to its nature, and inflicted upon it as punishment for obscure prenatal guilt, so that its main objective must be to free itself from these chains. A fortunate elect might hope to achieve this, and escape to the 'Banquet of the Pure' among the gods in the nether world – by priestly rituals of purification, incantations, and avoidance of certain foods, garments and situations, believed to have been prescribed by the mythical Orpheus. The collective thrust of these ascetic observances, which may at first seem rather trivial considered individually, was in fact immense, being no less than to instil a detestation of earthly life and satisfactions and a consuming will to withdraw from them. The unfortunate majority, being contaminated by neglecting these procedures, were supposedly doomed to traverse the 'Circle of Necessity' and revolve upon the 'Wheel of Birth', condemned to a hopeless succession of wretched earthly existences.

How then are we to explain this strong Greek propensity to mysticism, extolling the next life at the expense of the present one, pregnant with consequences for the future of Europe? The standard explanations, by no means incompatible with one another, are as follows. In the first place, it is held that Greek mysticism was mainly an import from Asia Minor or beyond, whence much of the mythological apparatus of later Orphism was undoubtedly borrowed, so that it was in Rohde's vivid phrase 'a drop of alien blood in the veins of the Greeks'. Then, there is E.R. Dodd's ingenious and more searching theory that it arose from consideration of dreams, of the fact that *in certain senses* the psyche is more active during sleep, when the body is quiescent.[24] This stubborn thought, it is suggested, made the Greeks identify the soul with this disembodied mode of experience, and thus it made them more vulnerable to the shamanistic cultures they encountered in Scythia, and probably also in Thrace, with their exaltation of the mentally dissociated initiate, as a repository of supernatural wisdom. Finally, we have the view that mysticism represents a natural, even inevitable, avenue of retreat in periods of acute political and social disturbance. Exponents of this theory rightly draw attention to a repeated association between upsurges of mysticism and this type of historic situation: the Pythagorean and Orphic movements with the turbulence of the sixth century, the comparable other-worldliness of Plato with the aftermath of the Peloponnesian war, and that of Plotinus with the troubled and anxiety-ridden ethos of the third century AD. It is well summed up in Festugiere's terse dictum, 'Misery and mysticism are related facts.'

Now, while all these theories may well point to real contributive factors and precipitants, they are surely altogether unsatisfactory as basic explanations. If proneness to mystical withdrawal was an infection caught through contacts with Asia Minor, we have to ask why the Greeks succumbed to it so readily, unless they were acutely susceptible in the first place, and why it came to play such an important part in their lives. Similarly, if it came from reflection on psychic liberty enjoyed in sleep, we need to explain why such a high value was attached to this part of experience – vivid and far-roving, but unsatisfyingly insubstantial, abnormally full of imagined rapid activity, yet mostly not informed by the truest kind of vitality – so that it was felt necessary to postulate, over against waking life, a special association with the soul. The last theory, that mysticism was necessitated by political distress, I believe to be the most implausible of all. A people tenaciously attached to nature and this present life would not have been so easily induced to desert them. To this final explanation of Greek mysticism, and the objection to it just made, we shall soon return, in connection with patristic world-rejection and contempt, often explained in the same way. As indicating likely favourable influences then, these suggestions are all credible and help understanding. But as fundamental answers to the problem they do not I think convince.

Rather, there is, I believe, a threefold radical connection between the intellectualism of the Greeks and their susceptibility to mysticism. First, from the conception of man's higher part as sovereign overlord of his lower, it is but a short and natural step to seeing the one as a divine alien imprisoned within the other, and thus to feeling the mystic exaltation of the soul to be a mere appropriate heightening of the hierarchical picture, no more than overdue promotion. For merely to *govern* the entire human organism is, from the viewpoint of enthroned and unassisted reason, an ascendancy not absolute enough. Nothing short of an *intrinsically superior status* will properly acknowledge its own sense of paramount excellence. Therefore, growth of the rationalistic spirit is almost bound to suggest to the intellect this further aggrandisement, although the timing may be determined by extraneous circumstances. Essentially, it is the same flattering train of thought that, in the political sphere, leads the despotic monarch eventually to claim not only unrestricted power but a unique connection with the deity. Next, in a rationalistic mentality, reason's subjugation of man's animal base eliminates the sense of an ever-fruitful association, thus removing the main objection to dispensing with the liaison altogether. In other words, the intellectualist Greek had from the outset but a slender and precarious attachment to his animal foundation. Lastly, and I believe most important, the same inner autocracy, by dividing man's integrity, stifles the central fulfilments which originate there, generating an intense frustration and melancholy,[25] for which a scapegoat must be found. What candidate for this role suits rationalism's book better than man's animal side, as represented by the body, which prevents unremittent rational activity? No other deprivation can be held accountable for such unhappiness, without calling in question rationalism itself. If man, being set above and apart from the rest of nature by his unique and supreme gift of reason, is nevertheless miserable, this can only be because he is denied, by his lower and physical component, scope for its unceasing exercise. All these quintessentially rationalistic lines of thought point to a jettisoning of ordinary and physical life, and a setting of the heart's longing upon a non-physical and in imagination far superior one.

Now these basic causes of Greek mysticism became no less operative in Christian minds, as the *rapprochement* between Christianity and Greek intellectualism progressed, and most potently so in the third and fourth centuries, as that union moved towards consummation. Thus, they must have been major factors impelling the fathers towards contempt for this world and preoccupation with a heavenly one. Such extreme concentration upon future betterment does not encourage the urge to ameliorate the present human lot, or the spirit of reform.

6

Hardly of less consequence here was a profound and similarly Hellenic elitism. The first Christian centuries saw a rapid growth of that typically Greek habit of mind which is radically consonant with rationalism's hierarchical bias and obsession with excellence, and is reflected both in Plato's confinement of the capacity for philosophic wisdom to the superior few and in the just considered Greek liability to mystical cults, conferring a blessed afterlife on a small band of initiates: the tendency to see the best things as esoteric mysteries, the preserve of a coterie of special beings, rather than as the common heritage of all. We recall how Plato identifies his minute class of destined philosopher-rulers with the tiny inner circle of mystics:

For 'many' as they say in the mysteries are the thyrsus-bearers, but few are the mystics – meaning, as I interpret the word, 'the true philosophers'.[26]

And we think of Sophocles' grim lines, to which I have just
referred, contrasting the happy fate of initiates into the
Mysteries, and the utterly wretched one of non-initiates:

> O thrice blessed they
> That ere they pass to Hades have beheld
> These mysteries; for them only in that world
> Is life; the rest have utter misery.[27]

Do not these words exactly sum up the attitude also of the
fourth-century Christian church towards the fortunate
minority within the fold, and the unfortunate great majority
without? Later, it is again distilled in St Anselm's belief that
'Few will be saved, and most of these will be monks'.[28] The
patristic craving for a small inner circle of the blessed, ringed
about by a vast waste-land of the doomed, is well summed
up by Peter Brown:

> One feature of late Roman society . . . is the slow
> emergence of a society ever more sharply contoured by
> religious belief. The heretic, the Jew, the Pagan,
> become second-class citizens. The bishop, the holy
> man, the monastic community rise in increasing prom-
> inence above the *saeculum,* the world of the average
> man. The community is ringed by the invisible frontier
> between the 'saved' within the Christian fold, and the
> 'damned' outside it.[29]

This impassioned elitism did not encourage a desire to relate
to ordinary mankind, felt citizenship of the 'great republic of
human nature', still less concern for the needs of ordinary
men.

For from this eagle's view of the average man as not fitted
for the highest fulfilments and ineligibly numerous too,
rightly shut out from the tiny magic circle of those who are
truly qualified, part of a finally despicable and dispensable
material order, and destined for a wretched future existence

properly reflecting all these disabilities, it is but a short and likely step to a fundamental indifference towards him, to regarding concern for his daily needs – in their own right, that is, rather than as ministering to beautiful and inward living which ensures salvation – as a waste of time and energy. The fathers were swift to take that small and probable step. Nor does this aerial perspective encourage a high regard for a prosaic contribution, upon which much of the ordinary man's well-being and happiness nevertheless depends, namely entry into public service. Accordingly, the fourth-century church tended to make Christians who took up this career feel that they were, if not sinners, then deserters of the highest ideals.[30] Similarly, it showed little real interest in the work of those were *were* public servants. In Jones's pointed words,

> The teachers of the Church offered no inspiring advice to a Christian governor. They urged him not to oppress widows and orphans, and not to pervert justice, but beyond such somewhat negative counsels they did not go.[31]

A deep care for the ordinary man would have led to more positive and far-reaching guidance. Finally, but by no means least, this whole complex of motives for withdrawal from mankind was immeasurably helped by the disruptive effect of patristic intellectualism upon human integrity, which prompts men to care for their fellows. The intellectualism of the fathers was even more severe than was general among the Greeks, for reasons that will be discussed presently. All these psychic pressures then contributed to fourth and early-fifth-century Christian inhumanity and indifference to the needs and distresses of ordinary men.

Insofar as they have been properly recognised, these last attitudes have generally been ascribed to a supposedly hopeless political situation, driving the fathers to abandon the earthly and human sphere; but that can hardly be their real origin. For one thing, despite the fathers' theoretical scorn for this world, their rejection of the earthly city, or final contempt for it as a mere stepping-stone to the heavenly (rationalised by systematic denigration of it, as incapable of true stability, harmony or completeness), in practice they showed a massive urge to gain power over this despised terrain, a paradox to which we shall return presently. As Brown again well comments:

> The Late Antique period has too often been dismissed as an age of disintegration, an age of other-wordliness in which sheltered souls withdrew from the crumbling society around them, to seek another, a Heavenly city. No impression is further from the truth. Seldom has any period of history littered the future with so many irremoveable institutions.[32]

He also speaks aptly of 'the blatant *Wille zur Macht*' of the period's ecclesiastical leaders.[33] This imperious temper of mind, so strangely at odds with the Master's command not to become like 'princes' and 'great ones', is reflected, for instance, in Ambrose's grandiose view of the sovereign sacerdotal authority and dignity of bishops. In a pastoral letter he writes:

> The honour and sublimity of bishops, brethren, is beyond comparison. If one should compare them to resplendent kings and diademed princes it would be far less worthy than if one compared the base metal lead with gleaming gold. For, indeed, one can see how the necks of kings and princes are bowed before the knees of priests . . . Nothing can be found in this world more lofty than priests or more sublime than bishops.[34]

The fathers certainly did not display in practice a despairing political quietism, and therefore cannot have been mainly motivated by one.

Nor was the political prospect, however inauspicious, so dire as to rule out hope in those disposed to be hopeful. We should remember here that the sack of Rome by Alaric in AD 410, although a grievous shock to confidence, did not lead to her immediate fall, or so weaken her resilience that Justinian could not reconquer Italy in the sixth century. It is significant too that Augustine's *City of God* was evidently planned well before the sack of Rome, a book on the two cities being promised in his earlier Commentary on Genesis,[35] which alone suggests that this calamity fitted and perhaps helped to precipitate it but was not an essential cause. And, when Augustine began this work in 413, he could look back upon the revived order and prosperity of the fourth century, the 'age of restoration', showing Rome's remarkable capacity to renew its strength. But above all the explanation has an inherent implausibility.We cannot imagine men tenaciously attached to nature and this world, such as the seventeenth-century Dutch, being driven to a philosophy of withdrawal and ascent just because of such uncertainties and external pressures as those besetting Roman society in the period concerned. Earlier, the same objection applies to the view that disillusionment at the fall of Athens caused Plato's retreat into a metaphysical scheme of fulfilment. Much later, it also invalidates one interpretation of the rationalistic poet Pope's growing distrust of the natural order, namely that it was due to the trauma of Tory defeat. Those who profoundly trust and love ordinary life are not so easily dislodged from their allegiance. Hence, the common belief that the fathers were driven to abandon the earthly and human sphere by political despair is surely a myth. Rather, they were so impelled by a combination of fundamental motivations, largely Greek in origin, and arising from their own Hellenic intellectualism, a complex of motives which must have made them half welcome a dark political scene, as a pretext for withdrawal.

7

HOLINESS AND THE HUMANE
RESPONSE IN THE AGE OF
THE FATHERS – II

1

Yet, however much they were given to preferring the theological level to the factual and human, and committed to a
Hellenic psychology and its proper aspirations, it is barely
credible that the fathers would have carried inhumanity so
far, flouting their Saviour's express command to love their
neighbour, without the presence of an even more powerful
factor: namely their passion for the Hebrew conception of
the Holy, a passion whose origin is the gradual fusion of
Judaeo-Christianity and Hellenism.

Before considering the effect of this commitment to holiness, we must briefly recall the historic process which led to
it and reflect a little upon the basic cause or causes of the
development. The union between sacralism and rationalism,
which was consummated in the fourth century, is ushered in
by the chequered, and partly temporary, convergence of
Greek and Hebrew culture in the late third and second
centuries BC. Notable expressions of this first *rapprochement*
were the Judaeo-Greek school of Alexandria, a new predilection for abstract and strictly rational thought and drive to
knowledge, the Hellenic quality of much Hebrew historiography and wisdom literature of the time, and certain Jewish
writers' scriptural adaptation of Hesiod's polemical centralist
myth the *Theogony*. But the most dramatic manifestation

was Antiochus' transformation of the Temple at Jerusalem into a Temple of Zeus Olympios, with the connivance of a Hellenising Jewish party in the city. Aristocratic Jews seem to have been attracted initially to Hellenism by wonder at the success and power and superior war technique of the Greeks, not their literary and philosophic achievement, which ties in with the Hebrews' previously noted prime motive for embracing centralism: the conferring of sheer strength and potency assisting territorial acquisition, rather than, as with the Greeks, a varied play of the higher faculties leading to many-sided excellence.[1] Moving to the next stage, eventual union is crucially eased and forwarded by the Alexandrian Philo (c. 20 BC - 45 AD), who turned the contents of the Bible, with much allegorical exegesis, into a Hellenistic philosophy, giving its revealed Creator an intellectual aspect and basis by uniting him both with the immanent ordering reason of Stoicism and the transcendent artificer of Platonism, which Philo managed to combine, through somewhat hazy thought and rhetoric.

Then, in New Testament times, the emergent fusion is critically advanced and symbolised by Paul's famous speech at Athens, addressed to a Greek audience whose centralism is largely sympathetic to his lofty and rabbinical mind, where he seeks to make the gospel intelligible and compelling in terms of their own modes of thought, by presenting his own Holy One, who is 'Lord of Heaven' and 'dwells not in temples made with hands', as a greater centre of power than their 'unknown god', and again when he preaches 'Christ crucified' to the Corinthians as another such superior sacral centre of potency, the power and wisdom of God. It likewise progresses when St John, probably both influenced by and speaking to the Stoicism blended with Platonism which was the philosophy of the average contemporary pagan, identifies his incarnate Word with the Logos of the Stoics and Philo. In sum, convergence is forwarded by the whole tendency of early Christianity to be partly a Greek philosophy of enlightenment, with a Hebrew sacralist emphasis.

At the last stage, a platform for movement to final union is provided by the second-century Justin, who is confident that Christianity and Greek thought are in essential harmony, that philosophy finds its consummation in Christ, that the world-soul of Plato prefigures the doctrine of the Personal Logos, and that Plato derived his concept of eternity from Moses' teaching 'I am the really existing', having learnt this while in Egypt. The work of Justin is continued by the brilliant Origen of Alexandria (*c.* 185–254), for whom 'the image of the supreme God is his reason',[2] and who sees Christ as tending the growth of Greek philosophy and ethics as carefully as he revealed the Law to the Hebrews. Finally, in the mind of Augustine there takes place an impassioned fusion of God as supreme Intelligence and absolute Holiness, so that no sooner has he praised him as 'eternal Creator of minds' than he also cries, 'Proceed in your confession O my faith, say to the Lord God, Holy, Holy, Holy, O Lord my God'.[3] Hence Augustine is able to set forth in the *City of God*, with all his ratiocinative and emotional power, a definitive synthesis of Judaeo-Christianity and Platonism, which he thus builds into the intellectual framework of Christendom. Tertullian might protest earlier, 'What has Athens to do with Jerusalem, or the Academy with the Church?'[4] but he sought to stem an irresistible tide.

We must next ask what fundamentally caused this union, or made it overwhelmingly natural and likely, if not strictly inevitable. In other words, why did Judaism and Hellenism converge so persistently over a long period? And why was Christianity Hellenised so completely, and so easily? To begin with the first question, we can only make sense of Judaism's steady fusion with Hellenism if we assume in it a radical kinship and welcoming frame of mind in the first place. Turning now to our second question, to speak fully to a predominantly Hellenic world, saturated with Greek philosophy and literature and education, Christianity had of course to adapt somewhat and accept the likelihood of some reciprocal influence, by seeking a common idiom and points of agreement, but not to capsize and denature itself as it did. Likewise, to refute alien Greek philosophies such as Arianism and Gnosticism, it had to use some of their language, but not to make this its own tongue, and go on speaking it long after the threat was past. In winning both these victories, it did not have really to be vanquished, absorbing more than it imposed. Rather, Hellenisation on such a scale is only intelligible if we again assume, in the Hebraic-Christian outlook, kindred and hospitable initial attitudes. And when we think of the profound resemblances between the Hebrew cult of holiness and the Greek one of reason, we see why these were indeed present. We saw earlier how the Hebrew outlook and the Greek are essentially cognate and compatible, mainly as both representing forms of pure centralism, similarly expressed and enforced by a lofty and anthropomorphic single or presiding god, but also through secondary common features: cults of excellence, a haughty and masterful distancing of nature, and the sin or hubristic offence, which justifies and enlarges a punitive deity. Because of this multiple deep affinity, it was suggested, an eventual marriage of true minds was entirely natural and probable, if not inevitable. Thus sacralism and rationalism in due time joined hands.

2

We are now ready to consider the effects of this conjunction, its psychic and moral repercussions in the fathers. Pre-eminently, it imposed a more absolutely centralised mental regime, and was humanely fatal. In the first place, it brought a new severity of intellectualism. For it dictated an alliance with the most pure and lofty late expressions of Greek rationalism, namely Platonism and Stoicism, and deified reason, by identifying it with the awful and remote Hebrew

Holy One. Conversely, it drove into final retreat, even if it could not eliminate, the benignly various and unruly elements in Greek religious belief and fantasy – such as the invocation of Aphrodite and Dionysus – by which the Greeks had to some degree preserved diversity of mental life and accommodated the irrational, just as it ostracised the broad and tolerant rationalism of Epicurus. Above all, it united the Greek tyranny of reason with the Hebrew one of will and exalted passion. Finally, the union of sacralism and rationalism further strengthened the ascendancy of this centralist psychology by adding the authority of a great religion and another formidable cultural legacy. Thus, as well as enforcing the thrust towards aggrandisement and inhumanity specifically associated with sacralism, it unleashed the full potential of pure centralism to disrupt human integrity, whence humane feeling flows.

It is this, surely, which best explains the extraordinary will to power which we noticed in the fathers, and found strikingly at odds with their rejection of or contempt for the earthly city, but still more so with their master's command not to become like 'princes' and 'great ones'. We saw in the Old Testament how a cult of holiness is embraced as conferring strength and potency, in the interest of dominion. For we noticed how the conception was harnessed from the outset to the gaining of territory and greatness, and led to an ever more ambitious expansionism, culminating in dreams of world conquest – either through other peoples' surrender to Yahweh or else through their annihilation. Hebrew sacralism also has a consuming intolerance missing from Greek rationalism, a psychic system which, seeking a diverse use of the higher capacities, is correspondingly better disposed to diversity elsewhere, and ready to regard some other races as barbarous Hellenes at heart, indeed even exceptionally to see some foreign customs as superior to the Greek, for all its elitist readiness to see the inferior multitude in a bad state. Thus, the sacralism of the fathers makes understandable their ferocious imperialism, of which it is surely an inevitable fruit. A cult of holiness releases a boundless will to power, whether or not embarked upon with that end in view.

More catastrophic still, however, the inhumanity of the fathers was consummated by the union of sacralism and rationalism, and given a final edge of fanaticism. The fathers hurled themselves upon the ascent to the Intelligible and Holy, conceived as a sublime unity. Accordingly, they consigned to outer darkness the unintellectual and unholy majority of mankind as unsuited to commune with these high conceptions, detracting from their absoluteness, and improperly numerous also. They turned Christianity into a centralist metaphysical scheme, at the expense of its message about life and conduct. But, most tragic, they stifled within them virtually all real feeling for the unfortunate, the slaves and the poor and the oppressed, as creatures of the same kind as themselves, passioned as they, cherishing the same incorrigible hopes of fulfilment, and not one whit less entitled to a place in the sun.

3

Thus, the fathers turned away from the last and most wonderful flowering of the Hebrew mind's organic underside, the teaching of Jesus, who bade men think of the sower going forth to sow, recall that every tree is known by its fruit, reflect on the fall of a sparrow, consider the lilies of the field how they grow; who commended in the tradition of Hosea the vitally connective image of God as father; who nevertheless cast his message within the conceptual framework of his time and place, which ascribed all good to a transcendent and loftily situated god, just as he accepted their messianic expectations, since not even major genius can step right outside the beliefs of its historic context, or communicate if it tries to do so; and who was duly rejected by sacralist Israel, while his call to greater wholeness was overridden almost at once by a logical and stronger craving for the Holy, like that of all Hebrews before him who sought to build upon the organic strand in Hebrew thought. The fathers also forgot the heart of their master's teaching, distilled in the story of a certain unholy Samaritan, who noticed a particular suffering fellow-man deliberately unnoticed by the holy, felt for his concrete distresses of being stripped and wounded and left half-dead, had compassion on him, bound his wounds, set him on his own beast, brought him to an inn and cared for him. In keeping with its logic, they left that endlessly fertile tale to speak first in its fullness to a much later age, which is often misleadingly called materialistic, and certainly had little time for holiness: the eighteenth century, which took it to heart notwithstanding, and slowly began to implement it on a proper scale. It is no accident that we have had to draw upon certain eighteenth-century writers on slavery and poverty to show the humane insufficiency of the fathers' attitude to these evils.

The commitment of the fathers to sacralism and its fruits was no new development. Most significantly, while the gospels contain only a tiny number of incidental references to the Holy, the writings of the rabbinical Paul abound with central and commanding ones – such as 'perfecting holiness in the fear of God', 'that we might be partakers of his holiness', and 'declared to be the Son of God with power, according to the spirit of holiness'.[5] To be precise about frequency of use, there are in the words attributed to Jesus no uses of 'holiness' and five of 'holy': 'Give not that which is holy unto the dogs', two apocalyptic allusions to the son of man's coming with the 'holy angels', a warning to 'stand in the holy place' on the last day of desolation, and a reference to God as 'holy father' in the theologically orientated St John's Gospel. Paul on the other hand extols 'holiness' eleven times, and uses 'holy' no less than twenty-nine times. Jesus speaks of the 'Holy Ghost' or 'Spirit' eight times, two of them being in St John's Gospel; Paul, twenty-two times. We should bear in mind here too that the orthodox gospel writers are highly liable to have slipped in the word 'holy' where Jesus never used it, and correspondingly

unlikely to have invented the neglect of it which emerges
from their account of him. But it is unsafe to place much
reliance on statistics here, because the gospels are a smaller
body of writing than the epistles of Paul, and contain much
more duplication. Far more significant, surely, is the
difference in emphasis. Whereas Paul's writings have a great
weight of commitment to holiness, in the recorded words of
Jesus the idea is barely stressed. More telling still, Jesus
substituted the injunction 'Be ye therefore whole, even as
your Father which is in Heaven is whole'[6] (and 'Be ye therefore merciful, as your Father also is merciful')[7] for the
sacralist 'Ye shall be holy, for I am holy' of Leviticus.* That
it to say, over against the aim of santification he enjoined the
soundness of being which, as we saw earlier, had been seen
as the inner kernel of the blessing.† Accordingly, the acme
of happiness and fulfilment is not to be holy but to be
'blessed', as we are insistently reminded by the great
succession of contained yet impassioned beatitudes which
opens the Sermon on the Mount. Indeed, the Sermon on the
Mount, which speaks so directly to the heart, is the culminating expression of the idea of the blessing.

It seems probable, however, that Jesus, like Hosea whom
we saw to use it only once, made *some* use of the word
'holy', and that again like him he never explicitly criticised
the notion itself. But, on the other hand, the life and moral
teaching of Jesus proclaim him the embodiment of resistance
in practice to the ideal of holiness and a sacralist way of life.
He fiercely denounced his religious establishment, their

---

* Lev. 11, 44. The standard explanation – namely that Jesus was simply dissociating
himself here from the negative and ritualistic misapplication of the idea of holiness
rampant in his day – seems to me superficial and inadequate.

† The Hebrew word *tamim* (the most obviously eligible to be rendered, in the Greek
of the N.T. record of Jesus's summons to entirety in Matt. 5, 48, as $\tau\acute{\epsilon}\lambda\epsilon\iota\circ\varsigma$,
most often misleadingly translated as 'perfect'), which occurs some ninety times in
the O.T. (e.g. Gen. 6, 9), signifies 'whole', 'entire', 'sound', 'without blemish';
while its corresponding noun *tom*, as we saw at the outset, is the one that denotes the
soundness or integrity which is the core of the blessing.

leading devotees and practitioners in his time; he challenged
the sanctity of the sabbath, its isolated and special status, by
justifying his disciples' eating of corn as they passed through
the fields upon it; he loved and esteemed children, who do
not naturally pursue holiness; he welcomed the ostracised
Samaritan woman at the well, so asserting the common
quality of human life and all that sustains it; and he received
the unholy tax-gatherer and harlot into the human fold.
When popular imagination pictured him as born among
domestic animals in a stable, an ordinary place where all
creatures are at home, and not a sanctified one, it caught the
essential spirit of his life and teaching in a wonderfully
precise image.

But all this could not avail against the entrenched ascendancy of sacralism. Of the Pauline weight of emphasis upon
holiness I have already spoken. In the Acts, the motivating
spirit is of course repeatedly called the 'Holy Ghost', and is
gradually elevated by early Christian thinkers into a third
divine person, identified with God's creative and inspirational power, so that by the fourth century Ambrose can
declare: 'There can be nothing which the Holy Spirit can be
said not to have wrought; it cannot be doubted that Angels
and Archangels, Thrones and Dominions, owe their existence to his operation'.[8] The late-first-century author of
Revelations beholds sacred beasts who cry day and night,
'Holy, holy, holy, Lord God Almighty.'[9] The early
Christian community prays: 'We give thee thanks Holy father
for thy Holy name, which thou hast caused to dwell in our
hearts'.[10] Another prayer composed within the first few
Christian generations runs:

Holy the God and father of all that exists,
Holy thou art who hast existed from the beginning,
Holy thou art whom all creatures know as God . . .
Holy thou art, and greater . . .
Holy thou art, and above all praise.[11]

An evening hymn in general use by the fourth century addresses Jesus as 'Holiest of Holies'.[12] The most solemn moment in the liturgy of the church is the Sanctus, although even as late as 400 its use was less widespread in the West than in the East.[13] So quickly does centralist holiness, with its principle of inner cleavage and divorce from ordinary life, prevail over even the most eloquent summons to increased wholeness, and a more communal vision of mankind, in minds where it is the endemic dominant, or that seek before all else a compellingly powerful and aggrandising religious idea; and above all in those which continue to worship the exalted god of the Hebrews, whose evolution was inseparable from his shaping prime attribute of holiness, so that this must ever and logically reclaim its dominant status in connection with him. The fathers, and those who followed them, only extended this inexorable process.

No attempt has been made here of course to give anything like a full and proper interpretation of the teaching of Jesus, which would require a book in itself. I have simply aimed to indicate where I believe the account just offered of the fathers stands in relation to that teaching, and the broad view of it to which I think this inquiry points. It is also one to which my own reading of the gospels has led me. If it is obviously an understanding of Jesus which treats him as fallible and therefore questionable, like the rest of humanity, it is also one that sees him as the supreme Hebrew creative genuis, whose moral thought is the climactic unfolding of the idea of the blessing, the richest and most fruitful ever conceived by the Hebrew mind.

8

HOLINESS AND THE HUMANE
RESPONSE IN THE MIDDLE
AGES – I

Finally, we turn to the humanitarian record of the Middle Ages, a matter on which the evidence is more meagre than we would wish. But, if far from comprehensive, it is also by no means negligible, and we can only seek to reach a just estimate on the basis which it provides. We should not affect a needless agnosticism here, still less feel that a sentimental idealisation should somehow prevail, until the contrary is proven. Equally, we ought not to brush aside the powerful religious impulse and framework of thought, treating them implausibly as a mere veneer on the surface of economic motivations.

1

To begin then with the Church, let us first consider the monasteries, where so much of its spiritual energies and wealth were concentrated in this period, and where distraction by secular commitments was least. The formative purpose of the monasteries was a saving retreat from the outside world, including ordinary humanity, a retreat through which the monk hoped to win for himself salvation, by purifying his soul in the service of God. It is true that these institutions also harboured aged bedesmen, periodically dispensed poor relief, often sent out an almoner to visit the infirm, and performed other such pious works of mercy as their rules and benefactions required. In certain places, such as Winchester and Abingdon, the monasteries also maintained hospitals that were mainly almshouses, not to be confused with the conventual infirmary, which did not receive outsiders. It has to be remembered here that some hospitals were integral with or directly controlled by a monastic society and staffed by its members, some separately endowed and merely placed under the administration of the monastery, whose members might or might not also staff it, while others had no connection with any religious house.[1] However, the leading founders of hospitals were, up to the end of the thirteenth century, kings and queens and a small group of bishops and noblemen, and in the fourteenth and fifteenth centuries, merchants and townsfolk.[2] Although some hospitals were founded by abbots and priors, abbots and their communities figure little in the muster roll of founders and benefactors.[3] They do not seem typically to have been active initiators in founding the hospitals attached to them.

But the evidence suggests that, even when medieval monks helped the poor and sick, they mostly regarded them less as cherished fellow beings than as accessories of the monastic ideal, instruments of the monk's central aim of sanctification, who at the same time served the sacralist vision by presenting monasteries as holy moral centres. The records of charitable giving to the poor, with their emphasis on festivals and numbers, have a chillingly ritualistic ring, suggesting a habitual neglect punctuated from time to time by pietistic bounty. For instance, of the great Benedictine abbey at Evesham, noted in the middle of the eleventh century for its charitable activity, we read that the abbot

> always gave bountiful provision from his own table to thirteen poor men daily. In addition, whether at home or abroad he maintained twelve poor men for the Maundy, who had food and clothing in all respects the

same as the monks . . . Likewise at Christmas, Easter, Whitsun and all the principal feasts, he gave presents of money to these and other poor people . . . Every year, four or five days before Christmas, and between Palm Sunday and Easter Day, a great army of poor and pilgrims used to come to Evesham . . .[4]

At Newminster, in the thirteenth century, a hundred poor persons received two oat-cakes and two herrings each on St Katherine's Day, while at Winchcombe a hundred poor people were fed on the morrow of All Saints.[5] Likewise, at Winchester, in the later Middle Ages, the monks of St Swithin's distributed bread six times a year, and the Almoner gave his old clothes to the poor once a year, instead of giving them back to the Chamberlain like the other brethren.[6] These and similar accounts give a strong impression that the poor were mainly brought in on special occasions, as agents of a religious scheme, and then largely forgotten.*

Even this peripheral humane activity shows a pattern of steady decline. For example, we read that the Abbot of Evesham's provision for the poor tended to disappear in the following century.[7] Special endowments for the benefit of the poor, which monastic communities also sometimes made, likewise tended to lapse. The abbot and brothers of Hyde set aside the revenues of the Manor of Alton (1080–7), by deed of gift, for the maintenance of the pilgrims and the poor. But William of Wykeham states in his injunctions to the abbey that the poor and infirm have been defrauded of their portion.[8] In 1301, the archbishop similarly has to

---

* Students of monasticism have commonly noticed, sympathetically or otherwise, the monks' meagre social interest and contribution. For instance, Capes remarks 'They did very little, in a word, for the service of the outside world' (*English Church in the Fourteenth and Fifteenth Centuries*, 1900, p. 288). Knowles observes, 'No work done within it [the monastery], whether manual, intellectual or charitable, is directed to an end outside its walls' (op. cit., p. 4). Significantly, too, in his monumental *The Monastic Orders in England* only 4 pages out of 780 are devoted to monastic work for the poor and sick.

insist that the brotherhood of St Peter's, Gloucester, should spend the proceeds of the Manor of Stanedisch upon the poor, as their rules provide, and not on general entertainment.[9] It was a common rule that the remnants of meals should be given to the poor at the monastery gate, but by the thirteenth century visitation reports are full of complaints that these broken meats are going not to the poor but to friends and relatives of the monks, or to the dogs.[10] The monastic houses also eventually often ceased to maintain properly even such hospitals as they were responsible for. By 1341, the hospital of St Lawrence, attached to the great abbey of St Augustine, Canterbury, was so starved of funds that it could not fulfil its functions properly.[11] The prior of Butley Priory withdrew the victuals from the leper-house in his custody, and reduced the revenues from £60 to 10 marks, and by 1399, it was said, 'the place where the hospital of old time was is now desolate'.[12] Later, when Edward IV travelled through Reading in 1479, he found that the abbot of Reading had destroyed his almshouses and appropriated the endowments.[13] In 1536, the prior and convent of Worcester suppressed the hospital of St Mary's, Droitwich, and 'expelled the poor people to their utter destruction'.[14] Why did apparently meagre monastic charity contract still further? Partly it seems to have wilted because it was always a feeble plant. The other half of the explanation lies in the rise of a rival focus of concern, the gratifications associated with wealth.

Before the early thirteenth century, when monastic unpopularity begins to deflect generosity elsewhere, wealth pours into these communities. Nobles and landowners endow monasteries apace, pious Christians are lavish with gifts and benefactions. Moreover, the monastic convert, who tended to belong to the land-owning class, gave his wordly goods away, commonly not to the poor but to his monastery. And so the members of these supposedly ascetic societies, founded with a view to forsaking the world for contemplation and apostolic austerity, become communal plutocrats, owning vast estates and identified with the aristo-cratic interest. If their ethical priorities had been different, the monks could surely have done much to avert the devel-opment, but they did not. Accordingly, notwithstanding reformist movements of which I shall say something in a moment, there sprang up a standard of living that vied with that of the neighbouring nobility, ranging from the moderately sybaritic, as reflected in Chaucer's monk, to the grandly so, as represented by the house of St Augustine in Canterbury, where in 1309 30 oxen, 200 sheep, 1,000 ducks, 965 fowls, 200 sucking-pigs and a quantity of mallard, partridge and larks were eaten at one feast.[15] Growing material comfort in turn attracted converts whose motives were not ascetic. None of this favoured a compassionate response to the poor.

Thus it comes about that we meet such robustly ego-centric figures as the abbot of Abingdon (1186–9), of whom it is related that, although immensely wealthy, he neglected to feed the poor in a time of grievous famine, or a later abbot of Evesham, who was so exploitative of his villeins that in 1369 he charged a tenant serf 20s and 8d for permission to employ his own brother.[16] Hence it arises that the monks of St Albans and St Edmondsbury strenuously resist the efforts of rural serfs to win their liberty, that monks use their influence with landowners to seize the advowsons of parish churches, and yield grudgingly to episcopal insistence on providing for a vicar, and generally fight for their privileges like landlords of the most reactionary kind. So it becomes all too understandable that, during the Peasants' Revolt, the tenants and serfs of great abbeys – such as Chester, Bury and Peterburgh – savagely attack them, which they would hardly have done if their inmates had truly befriended them, or been notable for pastoral solicitude. And, finally, this is why, when we consider the monasteries on the eve of their dissolution, we are struck by the very low proportion of their income that went to alms-giving: to be exact, almost certainly less than six per cent of their immense revenues, and the bulk of that, following the ritualistic pattern we have already noticed, on holidays and commemorative days or anniversaries of the deaths of donors.* But it had often been less. The accounts of Bolton Priory for the year 1324–5 show that out of a total expenditure of £647 10s 2¼d no more than £2 5s 4d was devoted to alms.[17] It has to be remembered here that, of monastic alms just before the dissolution, probably about a half on average were obligatory payments, from land bequeathed on condition that a certain proportion of the proceeds went to the poor.[18] It has been well said that 'Out of the dissolution could have come scores of schools, hospitals and generous endowments of the Universities, new highways, almshouses, and perhaps a major attack on poverty'.[19] Despite their periodic problems with taxation and debt, if the monks had been a socially concerned body of men surely they would have applied more of their vast wealth to some of these crying needs.

We must not forget of course that there were repeated reformist movements – the Cluniac, the Cistercian, the Carthusian. But we should not assume that the poor and unfortunate benefited from such reforms as took place. For the monastic reformers were concerned with bringing about stricter monastic asceticism, with restoring primitive austerity and devotional fervour, not with inaugurating a new charity. Thus, the main fruit of their endeavours was a proliferation of liturgical commitments, which left the monk with much less *time* for charitable work, insofar as he desired to undertake it. In the tenth and eleventh centuries, the saying of offices, which had originally taken up only a quarter of the day, often came to consume it almost entirely[20] – a change made possible by the increasing availability of serf-labour, which was in turn a consequence of the already noted growth of monastic wealth. At Cluny,

---

* See A. Savine, *English Monasteries on the Eve of the Dissolution*, 1909, p. 265. Snaith comments, 'But the charity of monks as revealed in their accounts gives us a very different idea of things from that in which some would have us believe' (*English Monastic Finances*, p. 118).

the main model and inspiration of renewed monastic life in Western Europe, no less than a hundred and seventy psalms were eventually sung by Cluniacs each day.[21] Whatever the multitude of the needy may have gained, in invisible terms, from the monks' unceasing orisons, they could only be losers, in concrete and immediate ones, from a near-quadrupling of these. The whole development seems to flow inevitably from an esoteric bias present from the beginning, which was bound to seek its own revival periodically, but could only tell against real social dedication. Still more to the point, these bids to restore spirituality did not more than briefly succeed, soon foundering on a stronger dynamic towards economic power and its rewards.

Medieval monasticism calls for both imaginative sympathy and realistic assessment, a respect for many who entered monasteries when they still offered an austere way of life and scepticism as regards these institutions and their value. The original ideal of a simple life of prayer, study and labour was genuine. It was not discreditable for sensitive souls to be attracted to a programme of withdrawal and ascent, when they were heirs of a sacrally heightened intellectualism which powerfully encouraged one, as we have already seen. That some men of conscience preferred contemplation to violence, often after first-hand experience of the violent life, was not ignoble. We can sympathise too with quiet natures who simply headed for monasteries as havens made for them. These and other impulses towards the monastic life we should acknowledge to be understandable, and often in some degree meritorious. Even so, I believe we ought to question the humane justification of the enterprise.

The principal humane rationale of the monasteries, like that of the monastic search for salvation, was of course belief in sin, acceptance of the Hebrew view that sinfulness is what is fundamentally wrong with man. It was the battle against sin which the monk felt to be his main social function, insofar as he thought of himself as having one, fending off from the land, but most of all from its rulers,

those devilish assaults by which the lure of sin was person-
ified. In the words of King Edgar's foundation charter for
New Minster at Winchester, referring to the abbot and his
monks, 'They defend the king and clergy of the realm from
the onslaughts of their invisible enemies'.[22] Extreme priority
was given here to emperors and kings because of their
supreme political importance, their supposed unique link
with the deity, and their great gifts to the Church.[23] At what
was thought to be a higher level, the monk also felt himself
to be socially contributive by discharging the penitential
debt of founders and benefactors, so preventing their sins
from causing their souls' doom, and doubtless he gave some
present peace of mind on this account.

But it was argued earlier that sin is a profoundly unhelpful
notion, mainly being an anti-organic idea that serves sacralist
centralism, which in turn leads to aggrandisement and
inhumanity, and continually tends to overwhelm the ethically fertile organic side of the Hebrew tradition. Surely, the
moral fruits of medieval monasticism bear out this analysis.
For never was more lovingly devised weaponry, in terms of
prayers and penances, directed against sin than in the
monasteries of the Middle Ages. And what came of it all? A
handful of much-loving and much-loved souls, it is true, but
there have always been such – and we do not know if they
became so because of or in spite of the monastic life. Yet
what seems mainly to have ensued is, even in the first more
inspired and dedicated phase of monasticism, humane con-
traction and retreat. All too soon afterwards there follows
the acquisition of vast wealth and possessions, then a slide
into venal self-indulgence and inertia, and even greater
humane indifference than before. Nor does the violent
crusading record of medieval rulers speak well for the
monks' attempts to guard them from sin.

The monastic contemplatives deserve that we should not
denigrate them, or deny their idealism where it was present.
But, above all, we owe them serious appraisal, which must
raise the possibility that they were psychologically and

ethically misguided, showed a lack of humanity and kindness distressingly at odds with their master's teaching, and
wasted human resources which were desperately needed
elsewhere. And the evidence suggests this to have been the
true situation. The medieval monk would hold that we are
using here a finally irrelevant criterion, judging his contribution in improperly mundane terms. Nevertheless,
remembering all the need and misery which he ignored, we
may well feel that we should apply that standard.

2

The dominant group of secular clergy, largely determining
the values of those below them, was of course the bishops.
The more important medieval bishops were immensely rich
grandees, preoccupied with running their vast and scattered
estates, involved in much litigation against neighbouring
landlords, and often embroiled in political administration
too, over and above their judicial functions. All this
inevitably isolated them from the mass of the poor and
greatly limited both their ability and disposition to help
them. The origins of the bishops' wealth and power lay far
back in history, in the episcopal situation under the
Christianised Roman Empire. At that time the bishop had
become an autocrat, whose position was assimilated to that
of the Roman governor. He was the sole authorised recipient
of endowments, which soon began to be generously
bestowed. Before long, he also received grants of land from
the crown, with the express intention that he should admin-
ister, on the monarch's behalf, a portion of his kingdom. Far
from resisting these opportunities to grow rich and mighty,
generations of subsequent bishops had jealously defended
them, and exploited them to the full. Thus, in the Middle
Ages, the wealth of the bishops was very great, and some
were opulent beyond most men's dreams. At the end of the
thirteenth century, the bishopric of Winchester carried with

it fifty manors and their revenues and an income of about £3,000.[24] The archbishopric of Canterbury had thirty-four manors, London and Exeter twenty-four, Hereford and York twenty-three. Canterbury, Durham and Ely all bore incomes of over £2,000.[25] We can gauge the enormous size of these figures by recalling that the average rectorial living was worth about £10 a year, while the bishops sought with mixed success to establish a minimum stipend for a vicar of £3 6s 8d, and assistant clergy received about fifty or sixty shillings a year. It has been estimated that the average English episcopal stipend represented about £300,000 in modern currency.[27] Such huge wealth was profoundly separative from the poor, and its retention scarcely compatible with deep feeling for their distresses. Episcipal revenues varied widely, however, and some were relatively modest. For example, the poorest of English sees, namely Rochester, was valued at as little as £183 10s 7d.[27] There is the same wide variation in France. Whereas the archbishopric of Rouen was taxed in 1470 at 12,000 florins, and the sees of Langres and Narbonne at 9,000 florins, the bishopric of Bayonne was taxed at only 100 florins.[28]

The major bishops lived in state and splendour matching their wealth. They had large retinues of officials and servants and a plurality of splendid residences, where they fed and entertained on the most lavish scale. During the fortnight 13 – 26 November 1289, Richard Winfield, Bishop of Hereford, and his household were at his manor of Bosbury, apparently without visitors. Over that period, in seven 'meat' days, they ate 6 carcases of beef, 5½ pigs, 21 deer, 53 geese, 60 fowls, 49 partridges and some ducks and pigeons. On the remaining days of abstinence, they consumed 2,000 herrings, 6 salmon, 19 congers, 225 eels, 200 lamperns, 4 hake, 1 cod, 1 stockfish, a quantity of freshwater fish, and some 2,500 eggs.[29] Small wonder that, despite their huge resources, many bishops fell into debt. The bishops followed their secular counterparts in enforcing the severities of feudal tenure. Even the exceptionally liberal Waynflete (1395?–1486) provoked his tenants into petitioning Parliament about his hardness as a landlord.[30] Sometimes bishops shared that typical obsession of great landowners, which so unfailingly alienates the humble, a detestation of poachers. In 1284, John of Pontissara, Bishop of Winchester (1282–1304), excommunicated certain persons for catching rabbits on his estate at Esher.[31] Many bishops were royal servants, heavily committed to household and ministerial business, or errands abroad, to the inevitable detriment of their role as pastors, and often even as Church rulers. Of the seventy-eight bishops who ruled in England between 1215 and 1272, twenty-two were so occupied.[32] How little in evidence many bishops were on the diocesan scene, let alone the parochial, is plain from the minimal demands made by the papal legate in 1268, namely that bishops and archbishops should be in their dioceses on feast days, and in Advent and Lent.[33] Minor bishops of the poorer sees, like Carlisle and Rochester, were rather better situated to be pastorally effective and keep close to their people if they wanted to. But, even when they used their greater opportunities, their influence was correspondingly small. The bishops' representatives and watchmen, the archdeacons, failed to redress their pastoral shortcomings, being mainly rich men or primarily scholars, with little interest in parish life or the poor. And the ever more notoriously lax and absent secular cathedral clergy, to be distinguished from the monastic but not sharply as regards their mode of life, copied their superiors on a smaller scale, but without their morally bracing great responsibilities. They present an image of plutocratic comfort and ethical torpor.[34]

There were of course caring and pastorally diligent bishops. Some outstandingly conscientious bishops tried valiantly to visit their parishes regularly, to be a father to their parochial clergy, and to instil in them a sense of their vocation. Hugh of Welles (d. 1235) devoted himself to improving the lot of the poorer parish clergy in his diocese of Lincoln; his successor the great Robert Grosseteste (d. 1253) strove to give his parish priests a higher conception of their pastoral obligations. But these efforts by a few represented an isolated moral *tour de force,* achieved against the main thrust of the episcopal situation and its formative values. A number of bishops founded hospitals, but this substantial charitable use of their wealth was likewise exceptional.[35] There were zealously reformist bishops too, who sought to raise pastoral standards by curbing clerical abuse in their dioceses. Archbishop Pecham (d. 1292) fought tirelessly to check pluralism in southern England;[36] Robert Grosseteste forbad it in Lincoln, in 1238; Simon of Ghent (1297–1315) tried to sweep it away in his diocese of Salisbury.[37] However, the example of England in the thirteenth century, with its handful of outstanding reformers, almost certainly gives too favourable an impression of bishops generally: for instance, we look vainly in Italy for their true counterparts.* In justice, it should be added, however, that truly scandalous prelates appear to have been a small minority, and that there were in the episcopacy many diligent servants of Church and State, grappling with the immense burdens of their office. Not a few bishops, for one reason or another, were honoured as saints, such as the gentle Hugh of Welles, and the fervently pious Philip Benini (1233–85), who never wanted to be a bishop. But none of this made up for the fatal deficiency of the medieval bishops: their uncritical commitment to a plutocratic style of life, utterly at variance with the teaching of Jesus, which estranged them from all the poor and humble in their care.

Not surprisingly, there was little love for bishops. Wycliffe calls them 'dumb hounds that may not bark in time of need',[38] and declares that a bishop without wealth regards himself as 'the bishop of nowhere'.[39] The poet Gower complains that the bishops serve two masters, God and the

---

* Brentano comments: 'The pastoral activities of the great majority of Italian bishops are hidden, if indeed they ever existed . . .' (R. Brentano, *Two Churches: England and Italy in the thirteenth century*, 1968, p. 183).

World.[40] And Jacques de Vitry (1170–1240) ascribes the evils of his time to 'prelates who are not sleeping but dead, not pastors but dissipators, not priests but pirates, who joined with wolves in despoiling the sheep'.[41] 'Is it not so', asks Gerson (1363–1429), 'that bishops today . . . are the officials more of the exchequer than of Christ, struggling tooth and claw in the courts of princes, and of secular jurisdictions, or of the Parlement?'[42] Such polemical critics are of course apt to exaggerate, yet their indictment usually presumes a basis of well recognised fact, and unmistakably so here because of its quantity and grave passion. Broadly, it must stand in this case: if medieval polemic against bishops gives less than the whole truth, it surely tells the main truth. Moreover, it is not the only kind of testimony to this effect. The fourteenth-century monastic chronicler Jean de Venette, who is no partisan controversialist, speaks with measured sorrow of 'the insensate pomp of bishops'[43] – and aptly too, for he seizes on the essential point. More than anything else, as has been indicated, it was their colossal wealth that was the humane and pastoral undoing of the bishops. This cut them off from the multitude of the poor and made a mockery of the Church as trustee of the gospel, while it encouraged the lower clergy to distance themselves similarly from their flocks, and from the teaching of Jesus.

3

The pastoral effectiveness of the parish clergy was crippled by the twin evils of pluralism and non-residence. There is some argument as to their precise extent, but general agreement that they were rampant.[44] In the course of the thirteenth century, pluralism became widespread.[45] By 1366, there were in the diocese of London alone no less than one hundred and seventy-nine pluralists, whose total income amounted to £7,500, an enormous sum for those days.[46] Pluralism reaches its climacteric in a figure such as Bogo de

Clare, son of the earl of Gloucester and Hertford, who by the time of his death in 1291 had amassed twenty-four parochial benefices, as far apart as Cambridgeshire, Northumberland and Ireland, two canonries, and three dignities in cathedral and collegiate churches.[47] Archbishop Pecham justly called him 'a robber rather than a rector'.[48] Most absentees and pluralists, of course, were so on a far more modest scale, yet it is significant that the system allowed a strong and determined operator to get away with so much. But Bogo de Clare is no isolated case. The royal clerk John de Drokensford (1309–29), while still under age, was Rector of Childwall, Hemingbrough, Kingsclerc, Balsham, Burton and Dalston, and held canonries and prebends at York, Salisbury, Wells, Dublin, Kildare, St Martin-le-Grand, Bishop Auckland and Darlington.[49] In the year before he became a bishop, Thomas Cantilupe (Bishop of Hereford, 1275–83) was rector of at least ten parishes, as well as Archdeacon of Stafford, Canon of Lichfield, Precentor of York, and Prebendary of St Paul's and Hereford.[50] This pastorally incapacitating piling up of benefices did not prevent his eventual canonisation. In the return, enumerating English pluralists, sent to the papal court on 13 January 1367, the richest pluralist listed is William de Wykeham (London), who draws an income of £873 6s 8d from thirteen scattered livings.[51] To swell his huge emoluments by a tiny sum, he does not scruple to hold a rectory in the Exeter diocese worth only £8, so depriving a parish of its priest.[52]

Certain bishops, as has been said, struggled against pluralism, but they were in a small minority, and often baulked by papal dispensation. Gregory IX, contemporary and friend of St Francis, issued as many as seventy-eight dispensations to English clergy to hold several benefices.[53] Reforming bishops were faced here with an abuse supported by mighty vested interests, deeply embedded in the social fabric, and upheld by the Church's relationship to it. Absentees and pluralists often had powerful kinsmen. A feudal episcopate, linked to the nobility by like values and interests, was in no position to challenge effectively a cherished perquisite of the aristocracy, a perfect way of providing for its younger sons, the less so since that aristocracy had itself endowed most benefices in the first place. Some bishops too were morally incapacitated here in a more personal way: they were themselves former absentees and pluralists, as we have just seen in the case of Thomas Cantilupe, Bishop of Hereford. Besides, the papacy was loath to lose its revenues from dispensations, perhaps inhibited too by its own practice of appointing relatives to rich livings, and sometimes protégés who were not even of age. And so, despite reformist bishops and the prohibition of pluralism by the Lateran Council of 1179, pluralism and non-residence continued to thrive, essentially on a basis of collusion by the higher echelons of the Church.

Yet the picture here is not wholly dark. Despite all this, there seems to have been at least a leavening of good and caring parish priests. It is this humblest of pastors, often scantily educated and owing little to European high culture, commonly united to his flock both by proximity and poverty, who seems most to have kept alive the image of the Good Samaritan. We must not idealise such parish priests as were resident. Robert Grosseteste speaks sorrowfully of 'the multiplicity of evils from which the people are suffering, owing to the negligence of their rectors, the carelessness of their pastors, and often (a subject for tears rather than a letter) the bad example and open wickedness of those who ought to be their spiritual guides'.[54] The womanising parish priest Pierre Clergue, brought to life for us by E. Leroy Ladurie in his *Montaillou*,[55] even if we do not know how typical he was, is likewise a valuable antidote against a falsely rosy picture. Nevertheless, greatly as parish priests must have varied in diligence, even when present, here was the one representative of the church whom Chaucer could unreservedly esteem:

> Wyd was his parisshe and houses fer asonder,
> But he ne lafte nat, for regne ne thunder,
> In siknes nor in meschief, to visyte
> The ferreste in his parisshe, muche and lyte . . .
> He was a sheperde and no mercanarie.

Such priests must have been common enough to be a recognisable type, if nearly always too obscure to win a place in the record, with the result that our knowledge of them is deplorably meagre.

4

It was largely in reaction against a scandalously wealthy and worldly Church, destitute of credibility and an affront to the gospel, that there arose the mendicant movements. The growth of towns, with their endemic liability to upsurges of spontaneous emotion, and their surplus of wealth available as alms, together with the mounting individualism of the thirteenth century, assisted them into being, while they drew strength from fear that the Church had lost authority and appeal for the masses, leaving a dangerous vacuum already beginning to be filled by populist heretics. The mendicant ideal was essentially renunciatory and ascetic – with a commitment to itinerant preaching, which had a higher priority for the Dominicans than the Franciscans – rather than charitable. Even with the more charitably disposed Franciscan wing of mendicancy, the central goal is an idealised and romantic religious poverty, in imitation of the self-pauperisation of Christ, not the relief of actual poverty. Like their forerunners the Waldensians and Humiliati, the early Franciscans flung themselves upon poverty as a spiritual citadel at once sublime and finally safe, an image of Christ's renunciation of the riches of divinity for a poor and obscure human life, and the one sure refuge from the blandishments of a corrupting world. It is to 'holiest poverty' and the 'eminence of loftiest poverty'[56] that St Francis summons his followers, and not a mission to relieve the ordinary distressed poor. St Francis bids the brothers rejoice 'when they find themselves among mean and despised persons, amongst the poor and weak and infirm and the lepers and those that beg in the street',[57] but evidently first and foremost as consummating friarly destitution, not because of the chance of improving these derelicts' condition. There is indeed considerable joyful acceptance of urban poverty, as a stepping-stone to high religious poverty. In essence, it is the old patristic preference of the theological level to the factual, somewhat softened and obscured by St Francis's rare combination of other-worldliness with tender nearness to ordinary men, whose twin origins seem to be his passionate devotion to Jesus and a feeling for nature quite unusually deep and immediate for his day.

In strict subordination to the aim of poverty, Franciscan mendicancy had of course a charitable aspect. St Francis lived among and helped lepers for a while; some continental friars followed him by working in leper-hospitals (although there seems to be no record of such service in England); the early Franciscans gave their goods to the poor on joining the fraternity, and we are told that they repeatedly gave their clothes or portions of them to beggars. But plainly this is only a sporadic and incidental philanthropy, without the main thrust of the Franciscan ideal behind it. And even this small credit balance is not without an adverse side: there is reason to believe that the respectable and fashionable mendicants made things worse for ordinary necessitous beggars, unintentionally encouraging a harsher and more niggardly response to them, by pre-empting the limited stock of generosity.[58] The lives of St Francis and his first followers are beautiful and moving, and we can only admire their courage and enthusiasm, but this must not blind us to their very limited humanitarianism. The most charitable form of mendicancy offered little to the poor, beyond the possibility of becoming poorer still, but in a more religious way – and it did not offer even that questionable help for long, because the friars' love-affair with poverty was so short-lived.

For the friars rapidly desert their founding ideals, astonishingly so indeed. St Francis had made abundantly plain his horror of the brothers' living in anything but the most makeshift settlements, commanding them to 'take nothing for themselves, neither house nor convent nor anything',[59] and even trying to tear down with his own hands a municipally provided house he considered too lavish.[60] Yet his death in 1226 is followed almost at once by the collection of funds for the sumptuous church and convent at Assissi, the abandonment of poverty made visible. Between 1228 and 1240 ten faculties were granted to rebuild or enlarge Franciscan premises, and between 1244 and 1247 over a hundred.[61] Soon the friars occupied houses as grand as those of the upper class. St Francis had held money also in abhorrence. In a special chapter of his rule of 1221, he had ordered all brothers 'not to accept coins or money in any form, either themselves or by an intermediary'.[62] Yet before long Franciscan friars are notorious like the rest as grasping legacy-hunters, 'fishers not of men but of money', as Matthew Parris called them in 1241.[63] The friars began by living on the very periphery of the social order, but were soon thoroughly co-opted into the establishment, becoming crusade-preachers and crusade vow-redemption collectors, papal legates and inquisitors, royal advisers and messengers. As early as 1234, Franciscans and Dominicans were the main papal agents for crusade-preaching. By 1239, Matthew Parris noted that they had 'become counsellors and special messengers of kings'.[64]

Many Franciscans even became eminent figures in the ecclesiastical power-structure, by accepting bishoprics, in perhaps still sharper contrast with what their founder intended. For we are told that, when St Francis and St Dominic met the Bishop of Ostia in Rome, the bishop asked them, 'Why do we not in future make bishops and prelates from among your brothers, who excel all others by their learning and example?' After imploring the bishop to keep the brothers in their lowly station, St Francis added, 'I pray you therefore, Father, that you by no means permit them to rise to any prelacy, lest they become prouder rather than poorer, and grow arrogant towards the rest.'[65] And yet within fifty years of St Francis's death, there are scores of Franciscan friar-bishops and archbishops, enjoying the estates and splendour of the offices. To be precise, forty-seven Franciscan bishops are known to have ruled in various parts of Europe between 1226 and 1261, with a dozen or so marginal candidates.[66] We should remember to the friars' credit their recurrent internal debate about poverty, but this does not alter the essential picture. After a brief moment as strangers and pilgrims on the earth, the friars forsook that way for aggrandisement.

5

Finally, the dissociation of the medieval Church from the poor and weak is vividly confirmed by the clerical chronicles of the time, which show an overwhelming identification with the great and powerful, that is to say the royal and aristocratic interests – together with an incorrigibly abstract vision, disruptive of human integrity, distancing from individuals and their concrete distresses, and consequently at odds with kindness. To begin with the first, the twelfth-century Giraldus Cambrensis, for instance, rhapsodises about Richard I as being 'incomparably illustrious', full of 'vigorousness and high-spiritedness', in other words a model aristocrat.[67] In like tones, he praises Richard's elder brother Prince Henry for being, in the right circumstances, 'more fierce by far than any beast'.[68] The *Opus Chronicorum* waxes lyrical about the greatness of Edward I, observing of his disposal at choice of the kingdom of Scotland, 'It is more glorious to make a king than to be a king.'[69] William of

Newburgh, writing of Henry II's running conflict with Louis of France, tells us that the King of France 'did nothing memorable in this war', but that Henry 'notably enlarged his borders'.[70] Similarly, the chronicle of Matthew Parris abounds with praise of knights, who are 'of illustrious race and renowned in feats of arms' and generally rich in knightly virtues. The historic heroes of the clerical chroniclers, then, are kings and nobles, seen from an unashamedly aristocratic angle and system of values. The present too is regarded from the same point of view. Protesting against the Lateran decree forbidding pluralism, Walter of Canteloupe complains that 'many nobles whose blood is the same as ours . . . will be driven into *ignominious* poverty'.[71] Thus, correspondingly negligible interest is shown in the great multitude of poor subjects whose distresses were not merely ignored but greatly aggravated by their aristocratic overlords, in their consuming passion for splendid possessions and conquests. The other main feature of the clerical chronicles, their abstract and general mode of apprehension – whose origin is the great theological, and intellectual, scheme of the Middle Ages – cannot be illustrated briefly. There is an intense interest in kings and nobles in relation to their status and roles, but an extraordinarily thin sense of human identity. As Brandt sums up the result of this generalised approach, 'The medieval clerk manifested very little interest in individuals because in a sense they could not exist for him.'[72] Nothing insulates us more from our fellows, and the sharp actuality of their sufferings, than seeing both through a veil of general conceptions, as Dickens brings home to us through his terrible Mrs General in *Little Dorrit*.

Apart from a few minor exceptions - the Chronicle of Jocelin of Brakelond, which is virtually confined to monastic affairs, and John of Salisbury's *Historia Pontificalis*, which shows some resistance to aristocratic values – the one notably original and dissentient clerical chronicler is the fourteenth-century French monk Jean de Venette. Though he does not question the established power-structure, he nevertheless shows an appalled recognition of aristocratic egotism and brutality:

> The nobles despised and hated all others and took no thought for the mutual usefulness and profit of lord and men. They subjected and despoiled the peasants and the men of the villages. In no wise did they defend the country from its enemies. Rather did they trample it underfoot, robbing and pillaging the peasants' goods.[73]

And he displays a pained awareness of the peasants' sufferings at the hands of the nobility:

> Every misery increased on every hand, especially among the rural population, the peasants, for their lords bore hard upon them, extorting from them all their substances and poor means of livelihood.[74]

This is not the kind of writing that stems from communing with abstractions. Rather, Jean de Venette's compassion is plainly rooted in an awareness of his lowly compatriots as particular fellow beings, and a sense of their concrete miseries. But his social concern and realism are shining exceptions, highlighting by contrast the prevailing attitude. In the main, the clerical chronicles of the Middle Ages sharply reflect the social sympathies of a Church obsessed with power and magnificence and made insensitive by its passion for abstract generalities.

The medieval Church, then, was not remarkable for charitable feeling and action, indeed it was staggeringly neglectful of them considering they lay at the heart of its master's message. For the most part, it was massively indifferent to the poor and distressed, who featured only peripherally in its thought and action, casualties of clerical dedication to grandeur and possessions, and to an abstract scheme. If succouring the weak and distressed is a prime function of God's representatives on earth, in combination with their commitment to worship, the medieval Church left that role for others to take up on a proper scale. It presided complacently over communities polarised between extremes of affluence and poverty, and was only too content to occupy the former. As Savine justly writes of the social response of the Church in the Middle Ages and later, 'In the hard struggle for life among its own children, it confined its energies to a policy of pious appeals to love and mercy.'[75]

9

HOLINESS AND THE HUMANE RESPONSE IN THE MIDDLE AGES – II

1

It is time that we paused to reflect upon the strange and distressing ecclesiastical pattern just traced, in which the most important figures are the bishops and monks, and to a lesser extent the friars. For the bishops dominated the life of the Church, largely determining the values of the lower clergy, while the monks were long held to be the practitioners of religion pure and undefiled, and the friars briefly held out the hope of religious renewal. The most constant characteristic of medieval bishops is their fierce will to power and wealth, to become and remain magnates, whatever the cost in alienation from the poor. It is stamped upon their deeds and achievements, as we have seen. And it is sometimes vividly reflected in their words. In the ninth century, Archbishop Hinckmar of Rheims declares,

> The world is chiefly ruled by the sacred authority of bishops and the power of kings . . . But the episcopal dignity is greater than the royal, for bishops consecrate kings, but kings do not consecrate bishops.

Anselm of Canterbury (1033–1109) affirms, 'I would not dare to appear before the judgement seat of God with the rights of my see diminished.'[1] As for the monks, the prime fact about them is that they soon slid into enjoying and stubbornly defending the privileges of economic power, and an aristocratic way of life, in the midst of crying need and distress. Not even a series of inspired reformers could arrest the thrust in this direction. Likewise, the friars rapidly move from holy poverty into a splendid style of life and complicity with the expansionist aims of popes and kings. How was it that men taught to find richness in utmost simplicity of life and an outpouring of pastoral care thus bent their main energies towards acquiring power and possessions? When we recall how Jesus commanded his disciples not to be like 'princes' and 'great ones', with their 'authority' and 'dominion', but to be ministers and servants, the repudiation of his teaching seems absolute.

Now the evolution of both bishop and monk is rooted in a historic and social context which partly explains it, and it is the same with the friar. The bishops had a proper pastoral interest in good and stable government, an interest which called for some co-operation with kings and a degree of integration with the feudal structure; and they could only defend their own in a world dominated by great men if they assumed a status of some magnitude. Moreover, being often chosen on political grounds, for secular administrative skills and experience or because of their ability to give presents and hospitality to kings in financial straights, they were bound to be unequally devoted to the Church and its mission. And their predominantly aristocratic origins made it easy for them to accept great possessions as legitimate.[2] As for the monasteries, since these depended upon the aristocracy for endowment and recruitment some movement towards aristocratic values was inevitable. Similarly, tradition weighed on the reformist friars, along with a felt duty to obey the Church establishment, and so did the tendency for institutionalism to overtake idealist movements as they expand. Yet, in all these cases, the deviation from Christ's injunction to embrace poverty and to care for the flock seems out of all proportion to what such factors ensured.

By no stretch of imagination, surely, did bishops need to become as rich as they did, if most were truly concerned to follow and serve their master, ever seeking to understand and apply his teaching more completely. As regards episcopal determination to be grand, the very contrary of what Jesus taught, no significant difference appears between more and less enthusiastic churchmen. If the monks' consuming desire was to renounce the world, could they not have avoided such vast territorial possessions and such complete infiltration by worldliness? Why was a goal of austere contemplation so vulnerable to mundane assertiveness and its rewards? As Southern pertinently asks of the reformist Cistercians,

> The Cistercian ideal demands complete self-abnegation, poverty, simplicity, retirement, purity and refinement of the spiritual life. But the historic role of the Order and its reputation among uncommitted contemporary observers suggest aggression, arrogance, military (or at least militant) discipline, outstanding managerial qualities, and cupidity. How is this contrast to be explained?*

By the same token, neither the force of tradition nor Christian obedience nor the pressures of institutionalism necessitated quite so rapid and complete a decline of the friars. Reformist movements often overcome such encumbrances. The bishops had, of course, their share of human frailty, and so did the monks and friars, but that hardly accounts for contradictions of such an order. Thus, the historic situation does not, I suggest, explain the staggering extent to which medieval churchmen pursued aggrandisement, at the expense of pastoral service and simplicity of life.

---

* op. cit., p. 252. Southern's suggested explanation – mainly that the Cistercians' success in increasing and improving their estates was held to be greedy by improvident aristocrats – does not seem to me satisfactorily to answer his penetrating question.

Nor can we plausibly ascribe it just to mortal weakness. There is, in a word, a 'credibility gap' here which we must somehow fill to make intelligible the gulf between original ideal and emergent practice.

It is not just an intriguing riddle that now confronts us, but a humanely vital question. As with most familiar parts of the historic landscape, we are apt to treat clerical obsession with power and wealth in the Middle Ages, the inhumanity of the medieval clergy, and the patristic surrender to these attitudes, too, with misplaced calm and resignation, just because we are used to knowing they happened. Not a little historiography also has made them seem un-extraordinary and morally neutral, treating them as data built into the socio-historical context, whose explanation need not be sought, and on which it would be futile to pass value judgements. These are tempting reactions, but surely altogether inadequate ones. The huge patristic and medieval will to aggrandisement, and shortfall of basic kindness, among serious and gifted heirs of two major civilisations, and a great religion, are in reality a truly appalling fact. There is something monstrous, as well as deeply perplexing, about the meagre humane response of the Church, not to mention its brutal inhumanities, in the centuries when it had things its own way. These phenomena demand that we fully register their enormity, acknowledge the size and urgency of the problem they pose, and then seek to understand them at a proper level, that is to say look for cause or causes proportional to such large and tragic effects. There is more here than a challenge to intellectual acuity. Even in the most remote and alien community, psychic and ethical disaster on this scale, in association with brilliance and high intent, combined with a seemingly almost ideal cultural legacy, would take us deeper than that. But these men are our none too distant predecessors. Their attitudes did much to shape our own culture and mental world; they remain significantly active within our present Western society.

To begin to understand properly what happened, I believe

we need to look back to the formative fourth century, with its church fathers who so paradoxically combine world contempt with imperialism. This seemingly contradictory stance, it was argued, stems logically from the marriage then of Greek rationalism and Hebrew sacralism. For the one breeds a craving for withdrawal and ascent while the other was adopted by the Hebrews as means to a like centralist psychology, conferring formidable strength and potency, such as in turn give advantage in terms of lands and greatness, which was harnessed from the first to territorial acquisition and aggrandisement, led to ever more ambitious expansionism, and finally generated boundless imperialist dreams. Medieval bishops and monks, and the friars too, were creations and heirs of this fusion of thought, and the unbridled *Wille zur Macht* that goes with it, just as they inherited and upheld correspondent social forms created in the fourth century, a great institutional and liturgical system designed to enforce its shaping vision. Soon or late, a cult of the Holy brings the old lust for dominion. Thus, holy fathers become empire builders; popes, claimants of temporal supremacy; bishops, princes; abbots, feudal lords; and ascetic monks, communally if not individually, owners of vast lands and wealth, while destitute friars soon enjoy ample possessions and influence. As well as emulating the fathers' sacralism, medieval clerics shared too – mostly in a changed form, of which I say more presently – their sacrally heightened intellectualism, with the devastating effect of both upon integrity, and so upon the kindness that flows from it, and which might have prompted them to draw nearer to the poor. The power-seeking clergy of the medieval period are far indeed from Jesus and his lowly disciples and those poor whose needs were at the heart of his message. But they are precise and faithful devotees of the patristic ideal, the one which had brought them into being and remained their prime inspiration. The bishops of the middle ages embody, like the popes who fought so tenaciously for temporal supremacy, the imperious spirit of Augustine and

Ambrose. The monks unfold within greater constraints the true logic and dynamic of holiness, though not what their founders had imagined would stem from it. And the friars' resolve to be poor cannot long compete with their psychic and religious system's thrust towards aggrandisement. Even all this is not enough to satisfy holy imperialism. Christian empire must be further extended by boundlessly destructive holy wars, those ancient fruits of sacralism, now called Crusades. That it is the humble parish priest, largely protected by scant education from both sacralism and intellectualism, who seems most frequently to have been a true pastor, appears to tie in with the whole analysis just put forward.

Seen in this light, surely the whole relation of belief to conduct here becomes coherent and intelligible, while we are also led to a truer picture of medieval churchmen. We are unjust to these often sincere and greatly aspiring souls if we suppose them mostly turncoats who betrayed their inspiration at the drop of a hat, altogether professing one thing and doing another, or mere puppets of socio-political and economic forces. In general, their religious intent was genuine enough, particularly at first. But their dominant aim was not to become Good Samaritans. Rather, it was to follow the fathers in pursuing sanctity and serving an exalted Holy One, in effect the path to a boundlessly expansionist centralism, even when not embarked upon with that end in view. To appreciate properly the controlling religious motive and aspiration is to make sense of the historic pattern, to understand the tragedy of the medieval clergy, and thus to see them in a more sympathetic light. Medieval religious idealism was essentially authentic, but it also unleashed, for that very reason, a devouring clerical will to power.

2

It remains to consider the humane response of the two other influential and homogeneous groups in the Middle Ages, namely the aristocracy and the new merchant urban elite, although we should remember here that merchants were sometimes of gentle birth.³ To begin with the first, the medieval aristocracy are *prima facie* improbable philanthropists. Men who casually slaughtered whole civic populations, greatly contributed to peasant unrest by hard seigniorial attitudes,* and often sent their daughters abroad at a tender age to marry men they had never met, seem unlikely to have shown much sensitivity elsewhere. Also, their humane horizons were limited by the honorific ethical system of feudal chivalry, obsessed with status and the proper aristocratic image, and dominated by abstract ideals, including 'largesse', but rating it well below the cardinal knightly virtues of 'prowess' and 'loyalty'. Knightly largesse, or generosity to inferiors, was essentially an inward-looking ideal, quite apart from its humanly insulating generality. As Brandt well observes, 'The conditions under which largesse was appropriate did not pre-suppose any sort of human relationship.'⁴ None of this, of course, rules out the presence in the aristocracy of charitable impulses, but emphatically it adds up to a climate highly inimical to them.

The charitable record of the later medieval nobility is in fact rather better than these factors would suggest, although not greatly so. No doubt this is largely due to fulfilment of social expectation, competition in conspicuous magnanimity, and above all the hope of a safe prospect in the next life; but we can only guess how much these factors contributed,

---

* Aristocratic oppression of the peasantry, and reciprocal peasant antagonism, in the later Middle Ages, come out strongly in Jean de Venette's Chronicle: e.g. 'They [the nobles] subjected and despoiled the peasants and the men of the villages' (p. 56). 'A noble hardly dared appear outside his stronghold, for if he had been seen by the peasants or had fallen into their hands, he would either have been killed or would only have escaped after rough handling' (p. 76).

probably often merging inseparably with a degree of charitable feeling. Much aristocratic generosity in the later Middle Ages was frankly self-regarding. A very large proportion of it went to endow charities, staffed by professional chantry-priests, the most certain way of ensuring the future of the donor's soul, as well as an imposing monument to him. There is a lamentable tendency for even gifts to the poor to be confined to paupers attending the donor's funeral, 'those present at my funeral', or lining the route of his funeral procession.[5] The custom of giving a basket filled with fragments of food after every meal to the poor at the gate, little more than a token gesture, seems overwhelmingly honorific in motive. Of wills making a considerable number of bequests, only one in three include money for alms.[6] Nevertheless, the later medieval aristocracy in England are known to have founded nine hospitals, nine colleges, and two university colleges (as well as fourteen monastic mendicant houses).[7] Unconditional, if usually very small, bequests to the distressed are also quite common, sometimes to the poor (usually the aristocrat's own tenants), sometimes for the relief of the sick or prisoners.[8] If the charitable contribution of the medieval aristocracy is unremarkable, it is not negligible.

3

But with the merchant urban elite, a group of men who tend to be sadly neglected and undervalued, probably because they are outside the high culture that is felt to be the glory of the Middle Ages, the case is strikingly different. We must not, of course, idealise the merchant class: doubtless, as with most medieval generosity, the safety of the donor's soul bulked large in their all too often posthumous charity, and sometimes this is blatantly so. The merchants are only a little less addicted to endowing chantries than the nobility. Commonly we find the same deplorable doles at funerals,

and funereal escorts of paupers, that abound in the last
arrangements of the aristocracy, while much mercantile gift-
giving to the poor is indiscriminate. Yet this is by no means
the whole story. In the later Middle Ages, the merchant class
seem already to have been the pioneers in such humanitarian
growth as occurred, as they were to be in the next period on
a much larger scale. They led the attempt to alleviate the
pitiful lot of prisoners without private means. About a
quarter of the wills of London merchants, in the later
Middle Ages, contain some provision for the relief of
prisoners.[9] Much of the wealth of the mercer Richard
Whittington (d. 1429), justly famous for his humanity in his
own day and a folk hero still, went to rebuilding and
enlarging the infamous Newgate prison, while by his benefactions he not only repaired St Bartholomew's Hospital,
but also added a refuge for women to St Mary's, Southwark,
and endowed the almshouse attached to St Michael Royal.
But Whittington's reputation rests partly too on donations
made during his life.[10] In a deed drawn up by his executors
after his death, he is called the 'worthy and notable
merchant, Richard Whittington, the which while he lived
had ryght liberal and large hands to the needy and poure
people'.[11] The merchant Stephen Forster and his wife
showed an interest during their lifetime in the beginnings of
prison reform.[12] Merchants and townsmen were the principal founders of hospitals in the fourteenth and fifteenth
centuries.[13] The example of the town of Anjou shows a
proliferation of charitable institutions in France, founded by
bourgeois urban laymen, beginning in the twelfth century.[14]

The merchants also display some real imaginative awareness of where social distress is most urgent, of which the
already noted concentration upon prisoners is one example.
A mercer bequeaths £25 towards providing free medical
attention for the London poor: 'I will that Thomas
Thorneton, surgeon, continue his daily besynes and comfort
of the poure sore and seek peple lakkying helpe and money
to pay for their lechecraft.'[15] Money is quite often left for

the provision of winter coal; one merchant gives £100 for disposal among poor fishermen and plowmen of the Sussex coast, because of their liability to suffer from French raids, another £702 to provide pensions for thirteen old people over sixty.[16] At the same time, the wills of medieval merchants commonly show a consciousness of the anxieties and impossibilities of poverty. Executors are often cautioned when collecting debts, not to do 'hurt or damage to any poure and nedy person'.[17] The mercer John Shelley instructs that his debtors in poverty are not to be troubled.[18]

But, most significant of all, some medieval merchants show a pained awareness of the *concrete distresses* of particular fellow men, the kernel, as was said earlier, of true and effective charity. The London mercer William Elsyng, who in 1332 founded Elsinge Spital, for the maintenance of a hundred poor blind men, declares that blind people 'tear at my heart'.[19] Thomas Knowles leaves money for piping the first water supply into Newgate and Ludgate prisons, 'consideryng alway the miserie and povertie of the prisoners that have no Rychesse nor liberte to pleyde neither complayn of their wrongs'.[20] Whittington charges his executors to rebuild and enlarge Newgate, because it is 'over litel and so contagious of Eyre, yat hit caused the deth of many men.[21] In the exceptional authenticity of humane feeling and pioneering charitable activity of the medieval merchant class, tentative as they are, we have the beginnings of the great outpouring of merchant generosity in the period following, already presaging its dominant role in the growth of humanitarianism then. These men are the forerunners of the enlightened and philanthropic merchants of 1480–1660, who contributed over 40 per cent of the charitable wealth of England, although they were a relatively small group, and who devoted 40 per cent of this to the needs of the poor, as compared with the higher clergy who assigned only 10 per cent of their charitable giving to the poor, concentrating instead on the more ecclesiastically relevant cause of education.[22]

Reductive explanations of mercantile charity have been offered by some historians. It has been suggested that the merchants were exceptionally alarmed about their prospects in the next life, either because their profession, and pursuit of money, lacked a religious justification, or because of their usurious gains, or because they could not be crusaders. While these may well have been contributive factors, as prime causes they do not convince. For one thing, there is no real evidence of the merchants' having in fact been peculiarly worried about their future state, as opposed to perhaps having theoretical grounds for being so. Nor does such abnormally acute anxiety tally with the worldly and buoyant temperament we associate with merchants through the ages, not in itself a conclusive argument against the above explanations but nevertheless an element in their failure to ring true. More serious, the incipient humanitarianism of medieval merchants is apiece with that of their successors in the following centuries, whose massive generosity, carefully vested in trusts and far-sightedly applied on a national scale, cannot even plausibly be ascribed mainly to pious self-concern. Above all, these unduly cynical explanations do not account for the perception of the most acute social evils, and plain distress at them, shown by some medieval merchants.

Rather, I believe it was mainly more positive factors which made the merchants outstandingly charitable for their period. In the first place, the profession of the merchant, constantly involving him as it did in the day-to-day life of the world, kept him in touch with the concrete needs and sufferings of his society, as loftier occupations mostly did not. But our argument so far suggests a more fundamental cause. The merchants were a consequential group relatively immune from both sacralism and sacrally heightened intellectualism. In the first place, their preoccupation with the mundane detail of trade militated against high-mindedness, a condition of thoroughgoing sacralism or intellectualism. Furthermore, they were mainly interested in reason only insofar as it was practically useful to them, while their usually limited education further shielded them from their time's prevailing psychic regime. As Sylvia Thrupp observes, 'The proportion of men in the merchant class who had stayed at school past the age of sixteen must have been very small.'* At the same time, the merchants were free of the humanely disabling encumbrances besetting the aristocracy, particularly their abstract vision and ethic, an intellectual construct, even if its adherents mostly were not intellectuals. Consequently, the merchants were the influential class least divorced from human integrity, the fountainhead of kindness, and least prone to abstract schemes that blight it at the root. It is no accident surely that St Francis and Chaucer, whose humanity and sane entirety are so exceptional in the later Middle Ages – with the result that we are apt to remember them at the expense of their contemporaries, even forgetting what most of them were like, and thus harbouring a most misleading image of the period – were both sons of merchants.

4

There were of course differences between the medieval and patristic centralist psychologies, fusing sacralism with intellectualism, as well as variations between individuals, to neither of which we can do proper justice here. But, broadly speaking, the growth of the secularist impulse from the twelfth century onwards (encouraged by the rise of a monetary system and consequent rapid economic expansion), brought an intensified rationalism, needed to implement the new secular ambitions, with a fresh stress on full human use of reason and a stronger tendency for it to dominate the actual cast of thought and the whole personality. The resultant centralism still incorporated a powerful sacralist

---

* Thrupp, op. cit., p. 161. As Thrupp points out, those who underwent a university education usually entered one of the professions.

component, primarily because sacralism remained substantially intact and dominant, but also because of continued
belief that reason is supremely embodied in the holy and
divine Intelligence, and a tendency to emphasise this more
strongly than ever, by way of countering misgivings that
unlimited employment of reason might be arrogant and
irreligious. The new rationalistic movement substantially
begins in the twelfth century. The early twelfth-century
William of Conches, profoundly interested in the universe
and in man, proclaims that 'the reason in everything must be
sought out'.[23] Peter Abelard (1079–1142) forges his instrument of dialectical argument, which he treats as the main
route to truth, and applies most memorably in his famous *Sic
et Non* ('Yes and No'), written in 1121–2. Adelard of Bath
extols man's wonderful gift of intellect, which 'examines not
only things in themselves but their causes as well and the
principles of their causes'.[24] The full expansion of the new
rationalism comes in the thirteenth century, with the
Aristotelean revival. Its leading figure is of course Thomas
Aquinas (*c.* 1225–74), whose *Summa Theologica* sets forth a
monumental synthesis of Christian theology and the thought
of Aristotle; whose association of the highest end of human
life, namely philosophical contemplation, with the divine,
makes his views theologically acceptable; and the practical
emphasis of whose moral thinking, with its stress on what
human individuals actually seek and can realistically achieve,
makes it ideally suited to accommodate and justify the more
worldly objectives of the time, particularly the mounting
preoccupation with honour and fame - values which feature
prominently in the ethics of Aristotle.

This is an age whose mental activity is marked by feverish
ratiocination and extreme cerebral virtuosity, both notably
uncontrolled by the human totality, and correspondingly for
the most part unfruitful – in the psychic and ethical sphere,
that is. As regards poetry, and science and mathematics,
the story is different. The other end-product of the new
rationalistic trend, a proliferating combination of idealism

and formalism, is well summed up by Huizinga:

> Now, a too systematic idealism (which is what realism
> meant in the Middle Ages), gives a certain rigidity to
> the conception of the world. Ideas, being conceived as
> entities and of importance only by virtue of their
> relation with the Absolute, easily range themselves as
> so many fixed stars in the firmament of thought. Once
> defined, they only lend themselves to classification,
> subdivision, and distinction, according to purely
> deductive norms.[25]

There are few surer paths to self-division, and disruption of
human integrity, than to think in these ways.

The new type of rationalism is evident in the thought of
all the late medieval philosophers. It reveals itself, on a
majestic scale, in the relentlessly systematising Aquinas, with
his ethic's imaginative and emotional thinness, its almost
exclusive stress upon intelligent action, as upon obedience to
law, and his justification of manifest inhumanities by
unimpeachable logic. Likewise, it is reflected in the excessively subtle thought of John Duns Scotus (1266–1308), and
in that of the inordinately scholastic William of Ockham (*c.*
1290–1349) (although his nominalist doctrine, defending the
claims of the particular against those of the universal, was in
principle valuable, even if confined to the realm of theory
and never really applied by him or his contemporaries). We
must not exaggerate the influence of scholastic philosophy:
the majority of late medieval Europeans were not among its
students. But, before making too much of this limited
readership, we should remember the disproportionate power
over events of the highly educated minority, who could not
fail to be affected by scholastic thinking. The result of all
this was an altered centralism, not less severe than the old, but
rather aggravated by a new will to think in a completely
rationalistic way, leading to the barren and radically
non-organic procedures of scholasticism. It was from this

changed and intensified centralist psychology that the merchants were comparatively exempt, by virtue of their anti-sacralist involvement in the worldly minutiae of trade, their mainly pragmatic interest in reason, and their mostly limited education.

5

It is often said too glibly, and with not nearly enough qualification, that we owe our humanitarian standards and achievements to Christianity. In a sense this is quite true, but in another it appears from our study to be profoundly false. To the innovative *moral* message of Jesus, most memorably expressed in the parable of the Good Samaritan, there is indeed an unreckonable debt. Even in the notably inhumane patristic age and Middle Ages, the ethical teaching of Jesus necessitated and sometimes inspired a certain amount of charitable activity, the more precious for being so exceptional: men hesitated to call themselves Christians without some implementation of it. It also gave rise to a small body of impassioned humane statement. But as regards the moral climate of society as a whole, which matters most to struggling mankind, it apparently cut little ice while combined with strong and operative Christian faith. The inhumane effects of sacralism, in alliance with Greek intellectualism, were the stronger force. Thus it seems to be quite otherwise with the *theological* teaching of Jesus, which stressed the organic and anti-sacralist notion of the fatherhood of God, but nevertheless lent itself, by its avowed continuity with Old Testament theology, to being logically taken over by a cult of the Holy, even though Jesus himself seemingly made light and sparing use of the concept. There appears to be in the main a negative relationship between humane feeling and a strong commitment to Christianity as a religious system. Leaving aside the primitive Christian age before the concept of holiness gained full ascendancy, humanitarian concern apparently wilts in believing and sacralist centuries, as our analysis of sacralism would lead us to expect.

Conversely, humane compassion appears to advance *pari passu* with secularism and laicisation. We have seen this incipiently during the Middle Ages, in the exceptional contribution of the worldly merchant class, which is still more marked in the following period. Looking much further ahead to the eighteenth century, we see that the major upsurge then of the humanitarian and reformist impulses comes at a time when men grow deeply suspicious of all high-flown aspirations, including sacralist ones; so that the parable of the Good Samaritan is much loved and communed with, while a watery deism enables most of them to be really philosophical benevolists, without the distress of feeling themselves no longer believing Christians. Why is all this so? It seems that the coming of secularism and laicisation restores to men, at first thinly and precariously, then more fully and surely, a proper hold upon their integrity, which sacralist and heavenly concerns tend to disrupt, while these also unleash an obsession with aggrandisement and with humanly insulating abstract schemes. Thus, there begins to flow that kindly feeling which is a function of entirety, and the pursuit of isolating grandeur becomes suspect, along with dehumanising great conceptual systems. Then men begin to be properly distressed by the poor and wretched, so that the moral teaching of Jesus takes on for them its rightful significance.

REFERENCES

CHAPTER 1

1   Gen. 16, 7–12; 21, 14–20.
2   Isa. 65, 8.
3   1 Kings 4, 29.
4   See Georg Fohrer, *Geschichte der Israelatischen Religion*, 1968, tr. David E. Green, 1973, pp. 66–74.
5   Exod. 15, 11.
6   I Sam. 2, 2.
7   Isa. 6, 3.
8   1 Sam. 6, 20.
9   For the influence of Sumerian myth on the Hebrew, see J.B. Pritchard, *Ancient Near Eastern Texts Relating to the Old Testament*, 3rd ed. 1969; Alexander Heidel, *The Gilgamesh Epic and Old Testament Parallels*, 1946; and *The Babylonian Genesis*, 1942. And for its probable indirect influence on Greek myth (particularly that of the *Epic of Creation*), see G.S. Kirk, *Myth*, 1970, especially p. 224. See also my *The Paradise Myth*, 1969, ch. 2, 'Themes in Sumerian and Greek Myth and Visual Imagery'.
10 See Thorkild Jacobsen, *The Treasures of Darkness: A History of Mesopotamian Religion*, 1976, pp. 6–7.
11 Jacobsen, op. cit., p. 9.
12 Gen. 15, 18–21.
13 II Sam. 22, 44; Ps. 18, 43.
14 Ps. 2, 8.
15 Ps. 135, 10–12.
16 Isa. 42, 8.
17 Ps. 29, 3; Ps. 24, 10; Ps. 145, 5.
18 Judg. 5, 31.
19 I Sam. 2, 8.
20 *Iliad*, V, 3–6.
21 Ps. 72, 8–11.
22 See A. Alt, *The God of the Fathers*, 1929, and Fohrer, op. cit., pp. 35–9.
23 Ps. 113, 6.
24 Jer. 20, 11.
25 Pedersen, op. cit., vol. 4, p. 531.
26 Ps. 96, 5.
27 See H.W.F. Saggs, *The Encounter with the Divine in Mesapotamia and Israel*, 1978, p. 39.
28 Gen. 1–2, 4a.
29 For a full discussion of the rise of the doctrine of Yahweh as world-creator, see Saggs, op. cit., ch. 2, 'The Divine in Creation'.

30   Josh. 10, 11; 1 Sam. 7, 10.
31   Judg. 2, 4.
32   Isa. 45, 12–13.
33   Ps. 136, 5ff.
34   Gen. 6, 5.
35   Ps. 51, 5.
36   Ps. 51, 3.
37   For a full account, see S. Porubian, *Sin in the Old Testament*, 1963.
38   Hos. 4, 6.
39   Hos. 4, 1.
40   Hos. 11, 1.
41   Hos. 2, 23.
42   Hos. 14, 5.
43   Hos. 10, 12.
44   Hos. 11, 9.
45   *Collected Poems of William Blake*, ed. Geoffrey Keynes, pp. 758, 348, 737, 289.
46   ibid., p. 480.
47   Jon. 4, 10–11.

CHAPTER 2

1   Ex. 20, 10; Deut. 5, 14.
2   Ex. 22, 30; Lev. 22, 27.
3   Deut. 25, 4.
4   2 Sam. 12, 3.
5   Isa. 1,3.
6   Prov. 5, 19.
7   Ps. 50, 10.
8   Prov. 12, 10.
9   Gen. 9, 9–10.
10   Gen. 9, 16.
11   Gen. 1, 28.
12   Gen. 9, 2.
13   Ezek. 34, 25.
14   Isa. 11, 7.
15   Ps. 8, 4–6. My italics.
16   *Antigone*, 332–52.
17   Ps. 104, 24–31.
18   Job 39, 6.
19   Job 39, 21.
20   Gerhard von Rad, *Theologie des Alten Testaments*, 1957, tr. S.C.M. Press 1975, vol. 1, p. 366.
21   Job 40, 18; 41, 5.
22   Exod. 19, 4.
23   Deut. 32, 11.
24   Jer. 48, 40.

25 Job 39, 27–8.
26 Prov. 30, 19.
27 Isa. 40, 31.
28 Amos 3, 8.
29 Hos. 5, 14.
30 Hos. 13, 7.
31 Hos. 11, 10.
32 Prov. 30, 30.
33 Num. 24, 9.
34 Ezek. 19, 3.
35 2 Sam. 1, 23.
36 Ezek. 10, 14.
37 Lev. 20, 25.
38 Lev. 11, 10; 12, 20, 23.
39 Lev. 11, 44; 20, 26.
40 See H. Ringgren, *Israelitische Religion*, 1963, tr. David Green, 1966, p. 142, and R. de Vaux, 'Les sacrifices de porcs, en Palestine et dans l'Ancien Orient' in J. Hempel (ed.) *Von Ugarit nach Qumran*, 1958, pp. 250ff.
41 A reproduction of the work will be found in Kenneth Clark, *Landscape into Art*, 2nd ed., pl. 94.
42 Gen. 7, 2.
43 Lev. 17, 14.
44 Deut. 22, 10.
45 The account given here of Hebrew dietetic law and its significance mainly follows that in Pedersen, op. cit., vol. 2, pp. 482ff.

CHAPTER 3

1   Ps. 68, 8.
2   Ps. 2, 6.
3   Isa. 52, 7.
4   Ps. 24, 3.
5   Ps. 121, 1.
6   Ps. 87, 1.
7   Isa. 42, 11.
8   2 Sam. 1, 19.
9   Ezek. 17, 24.
10 *Paradise Lost* 1, 6–15.
11 See J. Pedersen, 'The Role Played by Inspired Persons Among the Israelites and Arabs', *Studies in Old Testament Prophecy* (Robinson Festschrift) 1950, pp. 127–42, and G. Fohrer, *A History of Israelite Religion*, 1973, pp. 223–8.
12 Hab. 2, 1.
13 Ezek. 12, 17–20; 4, 4–8.
14 Gen. 28, 17.
15 Judg. 13, 6–7.
16 Exod. 23, 20–1.
17 Dan. 7, 1ff, 15; 8, 1, 15; 9, 1ff, 21; 10, 1ff.

18 *Compendium revelationum* (1495). See also P. Vasari, *Life and Times of Girolamo Savonarola*, tr. L. Villari, 1897, pp. 320ff.
19 *Idylls* VI, 10–14.
20 Ps. 42, 1.
21 Ps. 46, 4.
22 Ps. 23, 2.
23 Ps. 137, 1.

CHAPTER 4

1 Ps. 18, 27.
2 Ps. 107, 40–1.
3 1 Sam. 2, 4–8.
4 Deut. 24, 17.
5 Isa. 1, 17.
6 Pr. 13, 21.
7 Ps. 41, 1.
8 For the reforms of Urukagina, see S.N. Kramer, 'Sumerian Historiography', *I.A.J.*, 1953, pp. 217–32, and Maurice Lambert 'Les reformes d'Urukagina', *Revue d'Assyriologie et d'Archéologie Orientale*, 1956, pp. 169–84.
9 See S.N. Kramer, 'Urnammu – Law Code', *Orientalia*, 1954, p. 47.
10 *The Epic of Gilgamesh*, tr. N.K. Sanders, 1960, pp. 94–5.
11 ibid., p. 102.
12 Thorkild Jacobsen, *Towards the Image of Tammuz*, 1970, p. 80.
13 For these proverbs, see E.I. Gordon, *Sumerian Proverbs: Glimpses of Everyday Life in Ancient Mesopotamia*, 2.29; 2.30; 2.16; 2.19; 2.32. There are a number of other proverbs in the same vein.
14 From his *Essay on the Knowledge of the Characters of Men*. My italics. I am grateful to my friend K.E. Robinson for drawing my attention to this passage.
15 Isa. 45, 19.
16 Ps. 85, 13.
17 Isa. 1, 21.
18 Isa. 5, 7.
19 Isa, 1, 28.
20 Jer. 26, 4–6.
21 See Pedersen, op. cit., vol. 2, ch. 3, 'Righteousness and Truth'.
22 Isa. 5, 8.
23 Mic. 2, 2.
24 Amos 2, 6.
25 Mic. 3, 10–11.
26 Amos 2, 16.
27 Isa. 10, 16.
28 1 Sam. 21, 7; 2 Sam. 6, 10ff.
29 Lev. 22, 10.
30 Num. 1, 51.
31 Ezek. 44, 9.
32 Neh. 13, 23–25.

33 Ezr. 10, 3ff.
34 Num. 21, 2.
35 Josh. 6, 16–26.
36 Deut. 20, 16.
37 Deut. 20, 19.
38 2 Kings 3, 19.
39 2 Kings, 3, 25.

CHAPTER 5

1   See L.S. Mazzolani, *The Idea of the City in Roman Thought: from walled city to spiritual commonwealth*, 1970, ch. 5, 'Foreign Religions'.
2   N.R. Gottwald has shown this in his *All the Kingdoms of the Earth*, 1964. (p. 49).
3   Isa. 13, 16-22.
4   Jer. 10, 25.
5   Ezek. 25-32.
6   Ps. 2, 9.
7   Ps. 76, 3-12.
8   Ps. 2, 8.
9   cf. also Ps. 46, 48 and 89.
10 Exod. 15, 11.
11 Exod. 18, 11.
12 Judg. 11, 24.
13 2 Kings 5, 18.
14 Ps. 95, 3.
15 Ps. 82, 1.
16 Isa. 45, 5.
17 Isa. 2, 2-3.
18 Mic. 4, 1-5.
19 Isa. 9, 6-7.
20 Isa. 34, 2.
21 Isa. 14, 2.
22 Isa. 45, 22-5.
23 Isa. 40, 15-17.
24 Isa. 52, 1.
25 Isa. 49, 23.
26 Isa. 60, 10; 61, 5.
27 Mic. 7, 16-17.
28 Isa. 40, 9-11.
29 O. Eissfeldt, 'The Promise of Grace to David in Isaiah 55, 1-5', in *Israel's Prophetic Heritage*, ed. V.W. Andersen and W. Harelsen, 1952, pp. 196-207.
30 Hag. 2, 22.
31 Zech. 2, 9.
32 Zech. 2, 11.
33 Zech. 14, 9.
34 Zech. 14, 17.

35 Zech. 14, 14.

36 Isa. 61, 6.

37 In his essay, 'Nationalism-Universalism and Internationalism', *Translating and Understanding the Old Testament: Essays in honour of Herbert Gordon May,* 1970, pp. 206-7, and more fully in his four-chapter study, *The So-Called 'Servant of the Lord' and 'Suffering Servant' in Second Isaiah,* Supplements to Vetus Testamentum, vol. 14, 1967, pp. 3-128. Page references are to the latter work.

38 The four major sections in Deutero-Isaiah concerned are 42, 1 ff; 49,1 ff; 50, 4 ff; and 52, 13-53, 12.

39 Isa. 49, 2.

40 Isa. 42, 2.

41 Isa. 53, 5-6.

42 G. von Rad, *Theologie des Alten Testaments,* 1957, tr. S.C.M. Press 1975, vol. 2, p. 259.

43 Isa. 49, 6.

44 von Rad, op. cit., p. 260.

45 Op. cit., p. 27.

46 Isa. 42, 6.

47 Isa. 49, 6.

48 Isa. 43, 5-6.

49 In 'Nationalism-Universalism and Internationalism in Ancient Israel', the first of the two studies referred to above, (note 37).

50 Zeph. 3, 8.

51 Isa. 34, 2.

52 Nahum. 2, 1.

53 Nahum. 3, 1-7.

54 Nahum. 1, 15.

55 Ezek. 38, 22–3. My italics.

56 Ezek. 39, 2–7.

57 Ezek. 38, 16; 38, 23; 39, 7; 39, 21.

58 Ezek. 39, 17–18.

CHAPTER 6

1 *De Regimine Judaeorum ad Ducissam Brabantiae* (Aquinas: *Selected Political Writings,* ed. A.P. d'Entreves, 1948, p. 84).

2 Cited by Alastair Cooke, in *Alastair Cooke's America,* 1973, p. 189.

3 *De Civ. Dei,* xix, 15.

4 Ambros. Ep. 77, 6.

5 ibid., 37, 7.

6 *De Joseph,* 20; Ep. 37, 24.

7 *De Joseph,* 4.

8 Ep. 2, 19. For a fuller account of Ambrose's attitude to slavery, to which I am indebted for a number of the above quotations, see F. Holmes Dudden, *The Life and Times of St. Ambrose,* 1935, vol. 2, pp. 544–5.

9   'Melior est subjecta servitus quam elata libertas' (*Sententiae*, iii, 47).

10   op. cit., p. 978.

11   ibid., p. 979.

12   ibid., p. 934.

13   For a culling of such sentiments, see *Liber Scintillarum*, especially ch. 1, 'De Caritate', and ch. 43, 'De Misericordia'. I am indebted to S.A.J. Bradley for drawing my attention to this work.

14   *Rambler*, No. 53.

15   Ps. 41, 1.

16   In Ps. 41, 4–5 (my italics).

17   In Ps. 41, 1–2.

18   Col. 3, 2.

19   See A. Harnack, *The Mission and Expansion of Christianity in the First Three Centuries*, trans. J. Moffatt, 1908, p. 97.

20   2 Cor. 6. The only certain date in Clement's biography is that he wrote the first book of the *Stromateis* between 193 and 211. Strictly speaking, therefore, he may be held either a late-second-century thinker – or an early-third century one.

21   For an account of world-abandonment in the third century, see E.R. Dodds's fine study, *Pagan and Christian in an Age of Anxiety*, 1963, ch. 1, 'Man and the Material World'.

22   For the case against assimilating the Greek mysteries, in all but the most general terms, to *rites de passage* in other parts of the world, see Ugo Bianchi, *The Greek Mysteries*, 1976.

23   Sophocles, frag. 837, ed. Pearson.

24   See *The Greeks and the Irrational*, 1951, p. 140 ff.

25   See for instance S.H. Butcher's classic essay, 'The Melancholy of the Greeks', *Aspects of the Greek Genius*, 1891.

26   *Phaedo*, 69, c–d.

27   Sophocles, frag. 837, ed. Pearson.

28   R.W. Southern, *St. Anselm and his Biographer*, p. 101.

29   Peter Brown, *Religion and Society in the Age of Saint Augustine*, 1972, p. 14.

30   See Jones, op. cit., vol. 2, p. 985.

31   ibid., p. 984.

32   Brown, op. cit., p. 13.

33   ibid., p. 79.

34   Cited approvingly by Gregory VII in letter to Bishop of Metz, 1081. See *Documents of the Christian Church*, ed. H. Bettenson, 1943, pp. 148–9.

35   See J.C. Gay, *Unité et Structure Logique de la Cité de Dieu*, 1963, pp. 8–9.

CHAPTER 7

1　See M. Hengel, *Judaism and Hellenism*, 1974, pp. 12 and 31.
2　*Against Celsus*, IV, 252.
3　*Confessions*, XIII, 13.
4　*De praescr.* VII.
5　2 Cor. 7, 1; Heb. 12, 10; Rom. 1, 4.
6　Matt. 5, 48.
7　Luke 6, 36.
8　Ambr. *de Sp. S.*, ii, 5.
9　Rev. 4, 8.
10　From the 'Didache' or 'Teaching of the Twelve Apostles'. See A. Hamman, *Early Christian Prayers*, 1961, p. 91.
11　ibid., p. 63. This comes from the papyri, the orthodoxy of whose prayers is not above suspicion, but we have no reason to suppose it unorthodox, and in any case its interest does not depend upon its orthodoxy.
12　H. Chadwick, *The Early Church*, 1967, p. 274.
13　ibid., p. 266.

CHAPTER 8

1　For a full list of known medieval hospitals in England and Wales, indicating their secular or monastic status (and in the latter case their precise affiliation), and also their primary purpose, see David Knowles and R. Neville Hadcock, *Medieval Religious Houses in England and Wales*, 1971, pp. 310–39.
2　See R.M. Clay, *The Mediaeval Hospitals of England*, 1909, ch. 6, 'Founders and Benefactors'.
3　ibid., ch. 6.
4　*Chron. Evesh.*, 91–3. Cited by Dom David Knowles in *The Monastic Orders in England*, 1940, p. 482.
5　Fowler, *Chartulary of Newminster*, p. 108; V.C.H., *Gloucs.*, ii, p. 67.
6　Snaith, *English Monastic Finances*, 1926, p. 115.
7　Knowles, op. cit., p. 483.
8　W.W. Capes, *The English Church in the Fourteenth and Fifteenth Centuries*, 1900, p. 285.
9　Capes, op. cit., p. 285.
10　Moorman, *English Church Life in the XIII Century*, 1945, p. 357.
11　Clay, op. cit., p. 215.
12　ibid., p. 215.
13　ibid., p. 216.
14　ibid., p. 216.
15　Moorman, op. cit., p. 339.
16　*Chron. Abingdon*, ii, 293, quoted in Knowles, op. cit., p. 48; R.H. Hilton, *The Decline of Serfdom in Medieval England*, 1969, p. 38.
17　Quoted by Moorman, op. cit., p. 359.
18　Savine, *English Monasteries on the Eve of the Dissolution*, 1909, p. 265.
19　J.J. Scarisbrick, *Henry VIII*, p. 658.

20 See Lester K. Little, 'L'Utilité Sociale de la Pauvreté Volontaire', in *Études sur l'Histoire de la Pauvrete*, ed M. Mollatt, 1974, vol. 1, p. 449.

21 B.H. Rosenwein and L.K. Little, 'The Monastic and Mendicant Spiritualities', *Past and Present*, 1974.

22 *Liber Vitae*, ed. W. de Gray Birth, 1892, pp. 232–46. Quoted by R.W. Southern, *Western Society and the Church in the Middle Ages*, 1970, p. 225.

23 For the dominant position of secular rulers in the Cluniac liturgy, see Robert G. Heaton, *Crux Imperatorum Philosophia: imperial horizons of the Cluniac confraternities 964-1109*, 1976.

24 Moorman, op. cit., p. 169.

25 ibid., p. 169.

26 ibid., p. 170, conservatively adjusted for inflation.

27 ibid., p. 169.

28 P.S. Lewis, *Later Medieval France*, 1968, p. 302.

29 Moorman, op. cit., p. 178.

30 Capes, op. cit., p. 226.

31 Moorman, op. cit., p. 171.

32 W.A. Pantin, *The English Church in the Fourteenth Century*, 1958, p. 10.

33 Moorman, op. cit., pp. 238–9.

34 For a balanced and pessimistic account of them, see Capes, op. cit., ch. 12, 'The Cathedral Chapters and their Staffs'.

35 See Clay, op. cit., ch. 6, 'Founders and Benefactors'.

36 See D.L. Douie, *Archbishop Pecham*, 1952, pp. 104–11.

37 Moorman, op. cit., pp. 220 and 238.

38 Quoted by Herbert G. Workman, *John Wyclif: a study of the English Medieval Church*, 1926, vol. 2, p. 109.

39 Quoted ibid., p. 109.

40 *Vox. Clam.* Bk iii.

41 *Hist. Occid.* p. 270.

42 *Gersonii Opera*, ed. E. du Pin II (Antwerp, 1706) Col. 316, quoted by P.S. Lewis, op. cit., p. 298.

43 Chronicle of Jean de Venette, Trans., J. Birdsall, 1953, p. 86.

44 For findings which suggest that the prevalence of pluralism may have been somewhat overrated, see C.J. Godfrey, 'Pluralists in the province of Canterbury in 1366', *Journal of Ecclesiastical History*, XI, 1960, and C.J. Robinson, 'Beneficed Clergy in Cleveland and the East Riding', *Borthwick Papers*, 1969.

45 See Fliche et Martin, *Histoire de L'Église*, vol. 12, pt. 1, p. 574.

46 Pantin, op. cit., p. 36.

47 Moorman, op. cit., p. 26.

48 ibid., p. 27.

49 ibid., p. 29.

50 ibid., p. 28.

51 Godfrey, op. cit., p. 26.

52 ibid., p. 26.

53 Moorman, op. cit., p. 29.

54 *Collected Letters*, Letter 130, p. 440.

55 E. Leroy Ladurie, *Montaillou: Catholics and Cathars in a French Village 1294-1324*, tr. B. Bray, 1978, pp. 154 ff.

56   *Rule of 1221,* chs 5 and 6.
57   *Analekten,* ed. Boehmer, p. 10.
58   See Rosalind B. Brooke, *The Coming of the Friars,* 1975, p. 113.
59   *Rule of 1221,* ch. 6.
60   *Speculum,* ed. Sabatier, 1928, VII; II Cel. 57.
61   J. Moorman, *A History of the Franciscan Order,* 1968, pp. 118–9.
62   *Rule of 1221,* ch. 4.
63   *Chronica Majora,* Quoted by C.G. Coulton, *Five Centuries of Religion,* 1927, vol. 2, p. 171.
64   ibid., p. 171.
65   Thomas of Celano, *Vita Secunda: The Lives of S. Francis of Assisi by Thomas of Celano,* tr. A.G. Ferrers Howell, 1908.
66   Williel R. Thomson, *Friars in the Cathedral: the first Franciscan bishops,* 1973, pp. 1–20 and 150.
67   Cambrenis, *De instructione principum,* Disc. III, ch. VIII; *Opera Omnia,* ed. George F. Warner, RS. 21:8, 247.
68   ibid., Dist. II, ch. IX, RS. 21:8, 174.
69   *Opus Chronicorum,* in Saint Alban's *Chronicle,* RS, 28:3, 47.
70   William of Parvi, *Historia,* 5, xv; RS, 82:2, 456.
71   Matthew Parris, *Chronica Majora,* RS, 57:3, 418. My italics.
72   *The Shape of Medieval History: Studies in modes of perception,* 1965, p. 157. In this paragraph I am much indebted to Brandt's study.
73   *The Chronicle of Jean de Venette,* tr. J. Birdsall, 1953, p. 56.
74   ibid., p. 94.
75   Savine, op. cit., p. 267.

CHAPTER 9

1   Both quoted by Southern, op. cit., pp. 176 and 186.
2   For the aristocratic origins of most medieval bishops see Bernard Guillemain, 'Les Origines des Évêques en France aux XIe et XIIe Siècles', *Atti della quinta Settimana di Studio Mendola,* 1971, and Alexander Murray, *Reason and Society in the Middle Ages,* 1978, pp. 320–1.
3   See Sylvia L. Thrupp's fine study, *The Merchant Class of Medieval London 1300-1500,* 1948, ch. 6, 'Trade and Gentility'.
4   Brandt, op. cit., p. 109.
5   Rosenthal, op. cit., p. 104.
6   ibid., op., cit., p. 103.
7   ibid., p. 53
8   ibid., ch. 6.
9   J.A.F. Thomson, *Piety and Charity in Late Medieval London,* Journal of Ecclesiastical History, 1965, p. 185.
10 Thrupp, op. cit., p. 179.
11 T. Brewer, *Carpenter's Life,* p. 26.
12 Thrupp, op. cit., p. 179.
13 Clay, op. cit., p. 81.

14 See J.M. Bienvenu, 'Fondations charitables laïques au XIIe siècle', Études sur la Pauvreté, ed. M. Mollatt, 1974, vol. 2, p. 563.

15 Thrupp, op. cit., p. 179.

16 ibid., p. 178.

17 ibid., p. 179.

18 Thomson, op. cit., p. 185.

19 Thrupp, op. cit., p. 179.

20 ibid., p. 179.

21 Entry on Whittington, in *D.N.B.*

22 W.K. Jordan, *Philanthropy in England 1480-1660*, 1959, p. 348.

23 *Philosophia Mundi*, I, 23.

24 In his posthumously published *De eodem et Diverso* (Of Identity and Difference). See *Des Adelard von Bath Traktat De eodem et diverso*, ed. Hans Willner, Beiträge zur Geschichte der Philosophie des Mettelalters 4 (1903), no. 1, pp. 9–10.

25 *The Waning of the Middle Ages*, 1924 (1955 ed., p. 206).